SUPPORTING SKILLS FOR CARE WORKERS

Other titles from IES:

Keeping IT Together: Skills for Information Technologists
S Dench
IES Report 346, 1998. ISBN 1-85184-274-8

Exchanging Skills in Sales and Marketing
J Kodz, J Atkinson, S Perryman
IES Report 341, 1997. ISBN 1-85184-269-1

Productive Skills for Process Operatives
Giles L, Kodz J, Evans C
IES Report 336, 1997. ISBN 1-85184-264-0

Changing Roles for Senior Managers
Kettley P, Strebler M
IES Report 327, 1997. ISBN 1-85184-255-1

Trading Skills for Sales Assistants
Dench S, Perryman S, Kodz J
IES Report 323, 1997. ISBN 1-85184-251-9

A New Deal for Secretaries?
La Valle I, Giles L, Perryman S
IES Report 313, 1996. ISBN 1-85184-239-X

A catalogue of these and over 100 other titles is available from IES, or on the IES Website, www.employment-studies.co.uk

the **Institute**
for **Employment**
Studies

Supporting Skills
for Care Workers

S Dench
I La Valle
C Evans

Report 347

Published by:

THE INSTITUTE FOR EMPLOYMENT STUDIES
Mantell Building
University of Sussex
Brighton BN1 9RF
UK

Tel.   + 44 (0) 1273 686751
Fax   + 44 (0) 1273 690430

http://www.employment-studies.co.uk

British Cataloguing-in-Publication Data

A catalogue record for this publication is available from the British Library

ISBN 1-85184-276-4

Printed in Great Britain by IKON Office Solutions

The Institute for Employment Studies

IES is an independent, international and apolitical centre of research and consultancy in human resource issues. It works closely with employers in the manufacturing, service and public sectors, government departments, agencies, professional and employee bodies, and foundations. Since it was established over 27 years ago the Institute has been a focus of knowledge and practical experience in employment and training policy, the operation of labour markets and human resource planning and development. IES is a not-for-profit organisation which has a multidisciplinary staff of over 50. IES expertise is available to all organisations through research, consultancy and publications.

IES aims to help bring about sustainable improvements in employment policy and human resource management. IES achieves this by increasing the understanding and improving the practice of key decision makers in policy bodies and employing organisations.

Acknowledgements

The authors would like to acknowledge the help of all the employers and other organisations who gave up their time to share their valuable insights and experience.

Contents

1. **Introduction**   1

    1.1   Introduction   1
    1.2   Aims and objectives   2
    1.3   Research methodology   2
    1.4   Structure of the report   4

2. **Working With Children**   6

    2.1   Introduction   6
    2.2   A statistical overview   6
    2.3   What is care?   8
    2.4   A growth in demand   10
    2.5   The supply of childcare   11
    2.6   Pressures and changes   12
    2.7   Conclusions   18

3. **Working with the Elderly**   20

    3.1   Introduction   20
    3.2   A statistical overview   20
    3.3   Delivering care in different settings   23
    3.4   The changing demand for care   27
    3.5   Redefining the concept of care   28
    3.6   The wider context   31
    3.7   Conclusion   33

4. **Skills for Childcare**   34

    4.1   Introduction   34
    4.2   Basic skills   36
    4.3   Personal skills and attributes   37
    4.4   Physically caring for children   43
    4.5   A liking for working with children   45
    4.6   Understanding and managing child behaviour   45
    4.7   Knowledge and understanding of child development 47

	4.8	Administration and observation	49
	4.9	Equal opportunities	49
	4.10	Out-of-school childcare	50
	4.11	Managerial and business skills	51
	4.12	Changing skill needs	52

5.	**Care Skills for Eldercare**		**55**
	5.1	Introduction	55
	5.2	Basic level care workers	56
	5.3	Senior care workers	62
	5.4	Managers	64
	5.5	Changing skill needs	66

6.	**Recruitment and Shortages**		**69**
	6.1	Introduction	69
	6.2	Recruitment in the childcare sector	69
	6.3	Recruitment and caring for elderly people	72

7.	**Training and Development**		**76**
	7.1	Introduction	76
	7.2	Childcare	76
	7.3	Eldercare	78

| **8.** | **Conclusions** | | **82** |
| **9.** | **Bibliography** | | **87** |

Executive Summary

The Department for Education and Employment (DfEE) commissioned the Institute for Employment Studies to conduct a programme of work exploring employers' changing skill requirements within occupations. This report presents the findings of our study of two areas of caring: pre-school childcare and eldercare.

The study included: a review of existing literature; exploratory interviews with a range of key actors in these sectors; in-depth interviews with managers and proprietors in organisations providing care for pre-school children and elderly people; and a forum at which the research findings were discussed with participants in the study.

Working with children

Statistical overview

In 1996 there were just under half a million people employed in 'childcare and related occupations', around four per cent of the workforce. The sector has grown by 24 per cent during the last four years. The majority of these employees were women (98 per cent) and 65 per cent work part time. Temporary employment is also common, with 20 per cent of employees on some sort of non-permanent contract (compared to seven per cent of all employees). Average gross weekly earnings in childcare and related occupations were £189, just over half the average earning for the workforce as a whole.

What is quality care?

It is difficult to define exactly what is meant by good quality care, and indeed the minimum standards which are acceptable.

Definitions are bound to reflect accepted beliefs, and change over time. Fundamental to good quality childcare is the provision of safe and secure care for young children. Recently there has been a gradual move towards concern with entitlement, empowerment and advocacy. Debates have focused in particular on the ability of pre-school childcare to facilitate children's development, and there are differences of opinion about the type of development which should be given priority: physical, intellectual, social, emotional, moral, aesthetic and so on.

A growth in demand

There is a growing demand for childcare, stimulated by a number of factors, including: the increasing numbers of women participating in the labour market; a reduction in extended families; a growing number of lone parents; and, perhaps, a perception that participation in some form of pre-school activity has advantages for children. In particular, there is a growing demand for 'formal' sources of care. The breakdown of extended families and the unreliability of many informal arrangements have contributed to this.

The supply of childcare

Current levels of public provision of childcare in Britain are among the lowest in Europe. Furthermore, the provision of childcare outside the local authority sector has tended to evolve in a haphazard fashion. A private market has responded to women's need for childcare and a wide range of different types of provision have emerged. Employers have made a very small contribution. The voluntary sector has attempted to fill gaps in some areas, especially for families in difficult circumstances.

Pressures and changes

There have been a number of forces for change in the provision of childcare. These include:

- the 1989 Children Act
- Nursery Education Vouchers and associated desirable outcomes
- the government's consultation paper on work and family, and the more recent National Childcare Strategy

- the development of sectoral training targets, NVQs and National Training Organisations
- the Out-of-School Childcare Initiative
- development in the European Union.

All of these have implications for the future scale of childcare provision in Britain, the nature of provision, the type of care to be provided, and therefore the skills and training requirements of those working in the sector.

Working with the elderly

A statistical overview

In 1996, there were nearly half a million people employed as 'care assistants or attendants', representing two per cent of the workforce. The sector had grown considerably during the previous five years, by almost 50 per cent. Forty per cent of care workers were employed by the public sector and ten per cent by voluntary organisations. The occupation is dominated by women (92 per cent). Along with childcare, this is one of the lowest paid occupations: average weekly earnings were £182.

Delivering care in different settings

The level and type of formal care required by elderly people varies considerably and depends on their physical and mental conditions, as well as the availability of informal care. Different types and levels of care are provided in differing settings. Residential care is now only considered appropriate for very frail and dependent people, requiring heavy care and support. Lesser levels of care are provided in the community, at home and in day centres.

- *Residential care* — despite the move to care in the community, the majority of care staff are still employed in residential homes. The independent sector and private providers play an important role in this provision; local authorities now have a marginal role. Traditionally, staff have focused on the provision of personal care. However, there is now an increasing need for medical care, and for staff to play an active role in creating an environment in which clients' emotional, psychological and social needs can also be met. Residential work has been characterised by a lack of training and qualifications, low professional standards and poor development and career opportunities.

- *Domiciliary care* — a relatively new service which has been growing steadily since the 1940s. It is destined to expand further given the emphasis on care in the community. Traditionally, domiciliary care has been provided by local authorities, but the mixed economy of welfare has led to a growth in private provision. Voluntary organisations play a minor role. Domiciliary workers constitute a large army of women who are low paid and work part time. They are the most scattered group of care workers, and have a high level of responsibility and freedom. They are also isolated and vulnerable. In many ways they have a lower status than residential workers, and there are very few opportunities for training and development.

- *Day centres* — many day centres are run by local authorities and voluntary organisations. They now provide a range of activities and personal care, and provision is expected to expand.

The changing demand for care

The nature and level of demand for care for elderly people has changed considerably in recent years, due to a number of factors, including:

- demographic changes, resulting in a growing number of elderly people in the population. Elderly people also live longer, and are therefore now more likely to be frail, suffering from dementia and a range of other medical conditions typical of old age
- the increased participation of women in paid employment
- high levels of geographical mobility among young people.

These forces for change are also leading to changes in skill requirements.

Redefining the concept of care

In recent years, the way we think, talk about and conceptualise care has changed considerably, and this is leading to a change in the type, range and level of skills required of care assistants. Since the early 1980s there has been an ongoing debate about how and where care should be delivered, whose needs and criteria should be considered in planning the delivery of care and on issues such as quality, cost-effectiveness and ensuring equality in service delivery.

A range of themes and values are increasingly influencing these debates, and the planning and delivery of care. These can be summarised under the following headings:

- dignity
- rights
- empowerment
- choice
- fulfilment
- privacy.

The wider context

Recent legislative changes and government policy reflect these debates about the nature, type and quality of care provided to elderly people. The National Health and Community Care Act (1990) is the piece of legislation which has had the most significant impact on the provision of eldercare. However, other factors, outside the social policy framework, have also influenced recent developments. These include:

- more general ideas about accountability, quality and efficiency in the public sector
- the development of occupational standards and competencies has encouraged many care providers to examine their skill requirements and training needs
- recent health and safety legislation has led to a comprehensive review of practices and procedures in many areas of delivery.

Skills for childcare

Working with pre-school children in particular has been seen as a relatively low skilled occupation. Caring is often seen as an activity which is innate and comes naturally, particularly to women. However, our findings, supported by other studies, do suggest that childcare workers require a wide range of knowledge, ability and skills. It is not simply a matter of making sure the children under their care are safe, but of having a greater depth of understanding about children and how they behave, learn and play.

There were some variations in the expectations placed on childcarers working in different environments, for example, in a nursery, as a childminder or nanny, and at varying levels of responsibility. However, there were also many similarities.

The range of skills needed include:

- *basic skills* — literacy and numeracy are of increasing importance, especially as more record keeping is required and the educational content of pre-school provision is emphasised

- *personal skills and abilities* — a wide range of personal skills and attributes were reported to be important, including good communication skills; the ability to work with others and in teams; being reliable, committed, enthusiastic, organised, able to plan, punctual; maturity and experience; taking initiative; coping with responsibility; assertiveness; patience; flexibility; coping with change; learning new things; personal appearance. These are required in many jobs. However, it was the ability to apply these attributes and skills appropriately in relation to young children and their parents which was important

- *physically caring for children* — knowledge of health and safety, fire regulations, basic hygiene, nutrition, first aid and child protection issues; understanding what makes an environment safe for children

- *a liking for working with children* — not just simply thinking it would be a nice thing to do

- *understanding and managing child behaviour* — the need to understand the various approaches to managing behaviour, the advantages and disadvantages of each, and how theory and ideas are evolving

- *knowledge and understanding of child development* — theoretical understanding and underpinning knowledge of how children develop and how this has progressed over time, together with changes in the approach to managing child development. Those working with children need to understand current thinking, the reasons behind this and how this converts into practice

- *administration and observation* — partly as a consequence of the Children Act and the introduction of desired educational outcomes, there is a much greater requirement to observe and record children's progress

- *equal opportunities* — an understanding of what this means and how to operationalise the concept in practice

- *managerial and business skills* — including financial, budgetary and business planning skills, as well as knowledge of employment law and recruitment procedures. These are important for those who set up their own nursery or become a childminder. Those working as nannies and childminders also need to be aware of their own rights.

There has been a recent growth in out-of-school care, mostly catering for children between the ages of five and 12. Although some skill needs are the same, out-of-school care does raise a number of other issues. For example, the role of clubs in relation to homework; the need to provide a range of arts and crafts and sporting activities; meeting the emotional, psychological and social needs of a wide age range.

Changing skill needs

Greater thought and recognition is now being given to what it actually takes to provide good quality childcare. Emphasis is being placed on childcarers possessing a body of recognised skill and knowledge.

Our data also suggest that the role and job of a childcarer is changing. Those working in pre-school childcare have greater responsibilities than in the past, as life in general has become more complex; child safety, for example, has become a prime concern. There is also more scope to use theoretical knowledge underlying childcare, especially in promoting child development and managing behaviour. Many of the skills required are based on an evolving body of knowledge and information. Those working with young children, as in many other occupations, need to keep their skills and knowledge up to date.

Some of the biggest changes in recent years have been as a consequence of the Children Act and moves to increase the educational content of the pre-school curriculum. Literacy and numeracy in particular, but also other basic educational knowledge and abilities are increasingly important. Carers are also now expected to observe and record information about the children under their care.

Skills for eldercare

Basic level care workers

Basic care workers are almost exclusively involved in the direct provision of care. Relevant experience is normally looked for, educational and professional qualifications are not required. Respondents emphasised the importance of personal attributes and qualities, which must be evident on recruitment. These are different from the skills which can be learnt subsequently.

- *personal skills and attributes* — maturity, life experience and common sense are regarded as essential; an interest in people and an affinity with elderly people are also important. Other qualities sought include enthusiasm, motivation, having a sense of humour, sensitivity, tactfulness, patience and the ability to remain calm; flexibility, adaptability, initiative, reliability, honesty, and the ability to keep information confidential. Intuition was also considered important, being able to assess and react to people and situations quickly.

- *skill requirements* — these can be classified under four headings:

  - **personal care** — requiring an awareness of correct procedures for lifting and handling, bed moves, *etc.*; dealing with incontinence; preparing, handling and maintaining equipment used in personal care

  - **social care** — a more holistic approach to care places greater emphasis on social care and on responding to clients' emotional and psychological needs. This requires a wide range of knowledge, for example: an appreciation of the ageing process and its impact; understanding the needs of terminally ill patients and their families, and the bereavement process; an ability to communicate with a range of people, including clients, their relatives and other care professionals; an ability to organise activities providing mental and physical stimulation.

  - **medical care** — the need to provide basic medical care is increasing in both residential and domiciliary care. Those working in residential homes are increasingly likely to have contact with frail and infirm clients. Knowledge of common medical conditions affecting elderly people, on the use and abuse of drugs and first aid, are all of growing importance.

  - **domestic care** — traditionally the main requirement. Health and safety legislation has also changed the skills and knowledge needed. For example, skills include an awareness of food hygiene and handling, storing and using hazardous substances, as awareness of risk prevention and assessment.

Senior care workers

At this level staff start moving away from the provision of direct care, and their job is more about ensuring that care is provided according to organisational standards and procedures. They do not normally have line management responsibilities, but they are likely to be organising and managing other people's work.

Senior workers are expected to have all the personal attributes and specific skills required of basic level carers. They must have good oral and written communication skills, as reporting information is becoming an increasingly important part of their job. They must be good organisers, have basic administration skills, able to co-ordinate team work, able to delegate and judge whether or not other staff have the necessary skills and knowledge to carry out certain tasks.

Managers

The complexity of the work at this level can vary considerably, from the head of a small day centre managing a very small budget and group of staff, to the head of a residential home managing a budget of £1.5 million and a large group of staff. Relevant management experience is always required, but it is only in the public and voluntary sectors that this has to be specifically related to care.

The skills normally required in management posts are expected at this level. These include: a knowledge of personnel issues, good people management skills, leadership skills, financial skills.

Changing skill needs

Skill requirements are changing rapidly in response to recent legislative and cultural developments. An increasingly frail and older population requires more complex and heavier care than in the past. Personal care tasks are becoming more complex and the amount and level of medical care required have increased. Growing concern about workers' and clients' safety, and legal requirements, have also led to changes in skill requirements.

The shift to a holistic and client focused approach to care provision has reduced the emphasis on meeting clients' physical needs. More attention is paid to their emotional, psychological and social needs, and this requires a wider range of social, creative and interpersonal skills.

The need for care providers to survive in an increasingly competitive market is also leading to changes in the type and level of skills needed. In some organisations, flatter management structures have meant that basic level staff have to take on more and broader responsibilities. Some local authorities have expanded into other areas of care, including different types of provision for elderly people and meeting the needs of other groups. All these activities extend the range of skills required of care workers.

Gaps and shortage

Childcare

A number of gaps in knowledge and skills were reported. These included:

- the understanding and application of equal opportunities policies
- true understanding of child development and the role of play in learning
- relating to parents and families
- basic skills, in literacy and numeracy.

It was also reported that not all people keep up to date with changes in approach to looking after children, or see the changes made as important.

Eldercare

The main skill gaps were related to the cultural and legislative changes affecting provision, and the demand for more complex care. These gaps included:

- difficulty in changing staff attitudes; in particular, carers find it difficult to work with values, such as treating people with dignity, empowerment and allowing privacy
- an awareness of equal opportunities policies and practices
- a lack of understanding of some recently introduced key policies and procedures, for example the care plan and key working

- abilities in providing basic medical care
- literacy, particularly written communication.

Training and development

The majority of people working in caring occupations, particularly caring for the elderly, are unqualified. It has long been assumed that caring is an innate, usually female activity, which comes to people naturally. Training has therefore not been seen as very important. However, our evidence does suggest that this is beginning to change. A number of respondents reported that greater attention was being paid to training and development. Furthermore, the availability of training opportunities has improved in recent years, especially through the advent of NVQs and sectoral training targets. However, provision is still very patchy and a number of barriers to increasing training and qualifications were identified. These included a lack of resources and resistance to seeing training, particularly on-going and up-dating activities, as important.

1. Introduction

1.1 Introduction

The research reported here is part of a major programme of work commissioned by the Department for Education and Employment (DfEE), entitled the Skills Review Programme. The overall aim of this work is to explore how employers' skill requirements are changing within occupations. This complements other work conducted by, and for, the DfEE which reviews broad trends in the occupational structure of the workforce. The Skills Review Programme is a series of eight studies, covering the main groups in the Standard Occupational Classification (with the exception of the routine and unskilled occupations). The key focus is on the skills required by employers, how these requirements are changing and the main drivers of change. However, each study is broader than this, exploring training and recruitment, as well as any issues which are particularly relevant to the occupation in question.

Here, we present the findings of our study of the skills needed in two parts of the caring sector: pre-school childcare and elder care. 'Caring' was selected as one of the occupations for inclusion in the overall programme of research primarily because: it is growing in size and importance, it is in the service sector, it is heavily female dominated, and parts are traditionally regarded as requiring low levels of skill and few qualifications. However, caring covers a wide range of activities and we needed to focus on particular areas. Some caring occupations are regulated and have well established training structures, for example nursing, and it was felt that there would be limited scope in researching these.

There were many other types of caring which it would have been interesting to investigate, and it was decided to split the study to cover both childcare and elder care. This does mean that what was already a fairly small study in terms of the number of interviews, effectively became two much smaller investigations. However, although there is not much overlap between these two types of caring activities, there are elements of similarity of relevance to this study, as will emerge in the report. This study was conducted at a time when energies were being put into the establishment of National Training Organisations for different sectors, and when great emphasis was being placed on the specific training needs of different sectors. Our study does not attempt to repeat or replicate the research being planned or conducted as a result of these activities, but rather looks at current activities and needs within the occupations.

1.2 Aims and objectives

Each occupational study in the Skills Review Programme addresses a number of common research questions:

- What is the nature of skill requirements for the occupation?
- Have the nature and levels of skill requirements changed? Are the skill requirements increasing or decreasing? Are 'new' skills emerging and some 'older' skills disappearing?
- Which sorts of skill requirements are increasing and which are decreasing? Which are emerging and which are disappearing?
- Have the skill levels of the workforce changed to accommodate these changes? Or, have there been improvements in the supply of skills which have encouraged increasing skill requirements in jobs?
- Are the skill requirements for occupations likely to carry on increasing and decreasing? Do employers view change as a continuing trend?

1.3 Research methodology

There were four threads to this study of caring skills:

- a search of existing literature
- some preliminary exploratory interviews
- a series of interviews with employers, and
- a seminar to discuss and refine our findings and conclusions.

1.3.1 Exploratory interviews

A wide range of initial contacts were made for this study and we conducted a number of exploratory interviews. This was partly because of the large number of organisations with an interest in, and knowledge of, the two occupational areas. There was an additional reason for the childcare part of this study. The key focus of this whole programme of research has been employers' skill requirements. Defining an employer in the childcare sector presents difficulties. Although there are a large number of nurseries and playgroups, for example, many carers are employed directly by parents as nannies, while childminders are self employed. It was felt that an effective means of exploring skill requirements in this occupation would be to supplement our employer/manager interviews with a greater number of interviews with key players (compared to other studies in this series) in, for example, childminding and the training of childcare workers, to obtain a broader view of the skills needed.

Our exploratory interviews were with voluntary organisations, professional bodies, local authority associations, training providers, organisations involved in supporting carers, and others campaigning around various aspects of provision. Interviews were conducted with representatives of four organisations for elder care, and eight organisations for childcare. In three of these childcare interviews, we also explored more directly the skills required to do the job and how these were changing. These three interviews therefore double as exploratory and employer interviews.

These exploratory contacts and interviews had the following functions:

- to inform people about our study
- to identify any research which had already been conducted or was in progress
- to increase our understanding and knowledge of the occupation, and any key skill and training issues.

1.3.2 Employer interviews

The main stage of the research involved in-depth interviews with employers.

- Interviews were conducted with 16 training officers, personnel and senior managers in eight organisations which provided different types of elder care. Three social services departments, two voluntary organisations and three private providers were included in the study. These organisations provided a range of different types of care, including residential, domiciliary and day care.

- For the childcare interviews, the distinction between employers and other organisations was not always clear. Some organisations had multiple roles or were able to provide us with information on a group of care workers we would not have otherwise been able to include, for example childminders and nannies. We conducted interviews with nine respondents who were either managers of some sort of childcare provision, and/or who were able to provide us with direct information on the skills needed by those working in this sector (including the three which doubled as exploratory interviews). Our sample included: childcare provision run by local authorities, voluntary and commercial organisations, playgroups, nurseries, out-of-school provision and, indirectly, childminders and nannies.

All these interviews were conducted in the latter part of 1996.

The discussion guide

A discussion guide was developed to provide the basic structure for each occupational study. For this study, the discussion guide covered:

- background to the organisation
- changes affecting the organisation, and the caring occupation in particular
- the skills and abilities required of staff, and how these were changing
- external recruitment, and the identification of the necessary skills and abilities
- internal movement, training and development.

1.4 Structure of the report

The rest of this report is structured as follows:

- Chapter 2 provides a general statistical picture of those working in childcare, and looks at changes affecting the sector.

- Chapter 3 provides a statistical overview of those working with the elderly, and looks at factors influencing the provision of elder care.

- Chapter 4 discusses the skills needed to work in childcare and how these are changing.

- Chapter 5 discusses the skills needed of carers working with elderly people, and how these are changing.

- Chapter 6 looks at recruitment, recruitment difficulties and skill shortages for both occupations.

- Chapter 7 explores the provision of training for both occupations.

- Chapter 8 draws some conclusions and implications from our findings.

2. Working With Children

2.1 Introduction

This chapter provides a background to our consideration of the skills required of people working with pre-school age children. The information is largely taken from our review of existing literature, but also draws on some of our interviews. Looking after children has traditionally been regarded as a relatively low skilled occupation, something which comes naturally to people, especially women. This study suggests that this is changing. Although there is still a mass of unqualified and untrained childcarers, greater thought is being put into the skills needed and the training provision required to develop these. Indeed, there are a number of pressures and changes occurring which are adding impetus to this change. These include the provisions of the Children Act, the advent of Nursery Education Vouchers, greater emphasis on the educational and developmental values of childcare and a general growth in the sector. The chapter begins with a brief statistical picture of employment in childcare.

2.2 A statistical overview

2.2.1 Size and composition of the occupation

According to the Labour Force Survey (LFS), in 1996 there were just under half a million people employed in 'childcare and related occupations', making up around four per cent of the workforce. This sector has grown by 24 per cent since 1992, from just under 400,000 in 1992 to 490,091 in 1996. The types of jobs included in these figures are: nursery nurses, playgroup leaders, educational assistants and 'other childcare related occupations, which cover au pairs, child minders, nannies, playgroup assistants and playgroup helpers.

The vast majority of those employed in these occupations are women. In 1996, 98 per cent of employees in 'childcare and related occupations' were women (LFS, 1996). Four per cent of women in employment were in these occupations. The growth in employment between 1992 and 1996 has not changed the gender balance of employment. Childcare is, therefore, one of the most female dominated occupations and this is likely to persist. A recent study (Penn and McQuail, 1997) estimated that only one per cent of childcare workers were male. Penn and McQuail found that men were more likely to be perceived as potential paedophiles and this was helping to keep the profession largely female. Furthermore, they concluded that many women entering childcare saw the work as an extension of mothering skills, and that natural aptitudes were more important than training.

Childcare is not particularly dominated by any one age group. In 1996, according to the LFS, 21 per cent of employees were between 20 and 29, 31 per cent 30 to 39, 29 per cent 40 to 49 and 13 per cent were over 50. Many young people enter childcare, however it is also an occupation which many women return to after bringing up their own family.

2.2.2 Employment status and pay

Part-time working is widespread. In 1996, 65 per cent of women employed in 'childcare and related occupations' were employed part time, compared to 44 per cent of all women in employment. Temporary employment was also common, with 20 per cent of employees working on some sort of non-permanent contract. This is higher than amongst employees generally. According to the LFS, in 1996 seven per cent of all employees worked on a temporary basis.

Childcare and elder care (see Chapter 3) are amongst the lowest paid occupations. In 1996, according to data from the New Earnings Survey (NES), average gross weekly earnings in 'childcare and related occupations' were £189, this was just over half the average earning for the workforce as a whole. It was considerably lower than average earnings for all manual workers (£281) (ONS, 1996). The average weekly earnings for women in these occupations was £184. The number of men involved appears to be too small for the New Earnings Survey to provide separate information.

2.2.3 The extent of provision

In the course of our preliminary discussions we came across a number of attempts to estimate the scale of childcare provision in Britain (outside the school sector). What is interesting about these is the extent of difficulty reported in accurately measuring the extent of provision. It was argued by some respondents that existing estimates of the size of the workforce in childcare were inaccurate, and underestimated the number of people actually working with young children.

There is agreement that the childcare sector is large. A DfEE consultation paper (DfEE, 1996) reported that, in March 1995, there were over 1.1 million places for pre-school age children:

- 97,000 registered childminders providing 374,000 places. Three out of four childminders were registered for both pre-school and school age children.
- 5,500 day nurseries, including centres combining day nurseries and nursery classes, with 161,000 places.
- 410,600 playgroups offering an estimated two million children a place.
- 480 family centres provided by local authorities.
- 4,200 holiday schemes with 192,100 places (these also cater for school age children), (DfEE, 1996).

During the previous ten years there had been a large increase in provision. Between 1985 and 1995 the number of registered childminders increased by 66 per cent, and the number of places trebled. Provision in day nurseries also trebled during this period, although there had been little change in the number of places offered by playgroups. The pre-school childcare sector is therefore important and increasingly so, both in terms of the services it provides and the employment provided.

2.3 What is quality care?

A proportion of the literature on childcare discusses what care is and, in particular, good quality care. There are relatively few studies which specifically address skill needs. However, definitions of care and quality care provide an important background to any consideration of skill and training needs.

The quality of care is difficult to define. Tizard (1991) writes about the distinction between 'good enough' care:

> 'minimum standards to ensure that children are not harmed by the experience of day care'

and 'high quality' care:

> 'which would enhance their all round development and thus . . . involves education as well as care.'

However, what are these minimum standards and, once these are in place, what is good quality childcare? Moss (1991) argues that the answers to these questions are bound to be value-based:

> 'reflecting beliefs about what we want or do not want for children, parents, workers and local communities, all of whom need to be considered when attempting to define minimum standards or quality.'

Fundamental to good quality childcare is the provision of safe and secure care for children while their parents are at work. Meijvogel and Petrie (1996) suggest that with fewer safe places for children to play unsupervised, there is a growing awareness of the need for some sort of provision for school-age children and for recreational services. However, the principles of good quality childcare go beyond these basic factors. Moss (1996) argues that childcare services can and should have wider objectives than providing safe and secure care:

> 'they can and should provide children with opportunities for recreation, socialisation and personal development.'

He further argues that good quality services, in line with the emphasis on child-centred approaches, should be defined in terms of their ability to facilitate children's development. One approach to quality might be to focus on the child's experiences and the extent to which this experience enhances or hinders their development (Moss, 1991):

> 'good quality care is that care which is developmentally beneficial, while bad quality care is that care which inhibits development.'

There has been a gradual move in childcare towards concern with entitlement, empowerment and advocacy, approaches symbolised in the 1989 Children Act. However, there are still debates about what type of development should be given priority, physical, intellectual, social, emotional, moral, aesthetic and so on (Moss, 1991).

2.4 A growth in demand

There is a growing demand for childcare, stimulated by a number of factors, including:

- the increasing number of women participating in employment, education and training
- a reduction in the number of extended families
- growing numbers of lone parents
- and, perhaps, a perception that participation in some form of pre-school activity has advantages for children.

Recent research has shown an increasing demand for 'formal' sources of care. A 1991 PSI/DSS survey (Marsh and MacKay, 1993) found that 20 per cent of working mothers used 'professional' carers, such as childminders, nannies, au pairs and centre-based provision. They concluded that between 1980 and 1991:

> 'the proportion of working mothers using professional childcare has about doubled (and) given that the proportion of women working in paid jobs has also increased, the aggregate use of professional childcare has more than doubled.'

The results of a 1994 survey (Finlayson, Ford and Marsh, 1996) showed that there had been a further rise in the proportion of women using 'professional' childcare. These findings illustrate the growth in demand between 1991 and 1994. The proportion of working mothers using formal childcare had increased from 20 to 23 per cent. The proportion of working mothers using all forms of childcare, including family and friends, had increased over the same period from 63 per cent to 67 per cent. Sole use of informal care remained the most popular choice for about 45 per cent of working women.

The 1980 Women and Employment Survey (Martin and Roberts, 1984) found that the arrangements women make for childcare varied with the number of hours worked. Those in full-time employment were more likely to use formal and external types of care than those working part time. As the proportion of women working full time and returning to work full time after childbirth increases (McRae, 1991), it is likely that the demand for formal childcare will also increase.

The 1994 British Social Attitudes Survey found a considerable unmet demand for childcare, and this is repeated in other surveys. Four out of five non-working mothers said they would go out to work, and a quarter of mothers working part time reported that they would increase their hours, if they had the childcare of their choice.

The last few years have seen a major growth in the provision of out-of-school childcare, stimulated by the Out-of-School Grant Initiative funded by the (then) Employment Department through the Training and Enterprise Councils (TECs). A rise in female participation in the workforce has changed the role of the mother as primary carer of children outside school. In the past, grandparents, friends and other relatives were the main providers of this type of care. However, for many families this is not now an option. Family members no longer live close to each other and as more women enter the labour market, fewer female relatives and friends are able to provide this type of care:

> 'the supply of relatives able and willing to provide care, mostly grandmothers, is unlikely to keep pace with increased demand and is likely to fall eventually as more female relatives enter the labour market.' (Moss, 1991)

Informal care can also be unreliable and break down at the last moment (O'Brien and Dench, 1996).

2.5 The supply of childcare

The current level of public childcare provision in Britain is amongst the lowest in Europe (IRS, 1996). The provision of childcare outside the local authority sector has largely evolved in a haphazard fashion (Holtermann and Clarke, 1992). This has led to the private market responding to women's need to make arrangements for their children, while employers have made a very small contribution to the provision of childcare. The voluntary sector has attempted to fill the gaps in some areas, especially for families in difficult circumstances.

Formal care for under fives and school age children is provided by a range of different individuals or groups, including:

- nannies
- mothers' helps
- workplace nurseries
- day nurseries
- childminders
- out-of-school clubs
- crèches.

The Department of Health's review of day care services in 1991 found that between 1982 and 1991, the number of places at registered childminders increased by 140 per cent and at private registered nurseries by 264 per cent (Department of Health, 1992).

Cohen (1988 and 1990) and Moss (1990) concluded that the availability of childcare in the UK is limited by the lack of any statutory obligation on local authorities to provide childcare, except where children are defined as 'in need'. Less than ten per cent of children aged under four have places in any form of non-family childcare (Holtermann and Clarke, 1992). In the early nineties the education system provided places in nursery schools and classes for 25 per cent of three and four year olds, and places in primary school classed for a further 20 per cent of this age group (Holtermann and Clarke, 1992).

2.6 Pressures and changes

There have been a number of forces for change in the provision of childcare, these include:

- the 1989 Children Act
- Nursery Education Vouchers and associated desirable learning outcomes
- the government's consultation paper on work and family and forthcoming National Childcare Strategy
- the development of sectoral training targets, NVQs and National Training Organisations
- the Out-of-School Childcare Initiative
- Europe.

All of these have implications for the future scale of childcare provision in Britain, the nature of provision, the type of care to be provided, and therefore the skills and training requirements of those working in the childcare sector.

The 1989 Children Act

The 1989 Children Act sets the most recent legislative and quality assurance framework for pre-school childcare. It marks a major landmark in the history of pre-school services generally (Vernon and Smith, 1994). Although it left national policy in relation to levels of provision unchanged, it did set an agenda aimed at improving the quality of provision:

> 'The Government has, for **social** reasons, accepted a duty to ensure that day care (other than that provided informally and free) is of suitable quality and that young children are protected.' (DfEE, 1996)

The Act places considerable onus on local authorities to ensure that minimum standards of care are provided. For the first time, minimum standards were set for each of the different types of early childhood services in relation to child:staff ratios, room size and space, record-keeping, health and safety and discipline (Vernon and Smith, 1994). The Act also extended the regulatory framework for daycare to cover children up to the age of eight. Many of our respondents referred to the impact these provisions had had on their activities and, in particular, on the skills required of and expectations placed on staff. The Act also requires local authorities to:

- register daycare providers and monitor the quality of childcare in their areas
- make sure that children they identify as in need can go to a nursery, playgroup, childminder, after-school club or playscheme
- review the services in their area, listen to what other people think about them and publish a report
- assess the need for provision in their area, and
- consult with various bodies in planning how that need will be met. (DfEE, 1996)

In addition to the physical provisions of the Act, the Guidance accompanying it sets out six underlying principles. These principles set out what, perhaps, might be described as the beginning of a moral frame for the provision of daycare services for young children; a framework for the elusive quality discussed earlier. Vernon and Smith (1994) comment:

'The Guidance accompanying the Act therefore sets out six general principals which, it states, should underpin all day care, education and related services for young children and their families, these being:

- children's welfare and development be paramount
- children should be treated and respected as individuals whose needs (including special educational needs) should be catered for
- parents' responsibility for their children should be recognised and respected
- the values deriving from different backgrounds — ethnic, cultural, religious and linguistic — should be recognised and respected
- parents are generally the first educators of their children; this should be reflected in their relationships with other carers and providers
- parents should have easy access to information about services in their area and be able to make informed choices.'

Pugh (1992) and Vernon and Smith (1994) discuss how the Act goes further than any other previous government guidance. In particular, through addressing curriculum issues, equal opportunities and matters relating to parental involvement. Concern was, however, expressed about the chances of these aspects of the Act being implemented:

'The curriculum, equal opportunities and parental involvement all challenge traditional modes of operating (if not thinking) and as such entail cultural change which will necessitate ongoing training and resources . . . the Act itself makes no provision for this.' (Vernon and Smith, 1994)

Elfer and Beasley (1997) also comment on the enthusiasm with which the 1989 Children Act was greeted:

'It offered a new regulatory framework unified into the main-stream of children's legislation . . . . The Department [of Health] also commissioned dedicated training materials for registration and inspection officers and most had at least one, and many six, full days of training to prepare for implementation . . ., there was optimism about the new regulatory framework and the *commitment from central government to its effective implementation.'*

There can be no doubt that the 1989 Children Act has had an impact on some areas of provision. Many of the people we spoke to in the course of the study referred to it having at least a minimum impact on activities. However, we were interviewing amongst what might be regarded as 'good practice' providers and those working to improve the skills and professionalism of carers. A recent examination of appeals under Part X of the Children Act (Elfer and Beasley, 1997) concluded:

> *'Thus regulation is working to the extent that it does appear to ensure that most children are protected from danger arising from lack of physical safety or from people who would abuse or injure them. Regulation also works in that the legislation, together with the detailed accompanying guidance on standards, provides a framework, which facilitates the development and negotiation of standards with providers willing to work within this framework. But according to the evidence of this survey, regulation is not working to reliably protect children and families from providers who persistently seek to evade and dilute standards ... the survey found very little evidence of formal action in relation to supporting standards concerning each child's needs arising from their religious persuasion, racial origin and cultural and linguistic background.'*

At the time of finalising this report, a draft National Childcare Strategy was about to be published. This will no doubt go further in developing a regulatory framework for the provision of care for young children. Providing good quality and available childcare is a major priority for the current administration. Pressures on providers and those working with children to improve the quality of service, and hence their own skills, are likely to continue.

Nursery Education Vouchers and the educational content of pre-school provision

At the time this research was conducted a major concern amongst providers was the potential impact of Nursery Education Vouchers. To qualify and offer places under this initiative, providers of pre-school childcare for four year olds had to be able to show an ability to meet the 'desired learning outcomes'. This was effectively increasing the educational content of pre-school childcare, and creating a demand for different skills from those working in this sector. Since then, the election of a Labour government has resulted in the abandonment of Nursery Education Vouchers. However, there remains a continued emphasis on the educational content of pre-school childcare.

Government consultations

At the time of our interviews the Department for Education and Employment had recently published a consultation paper (DfEE, 1996). This set out a suggested agenda for change, based around the development of a policy framework which addressed issues of availability, affordability, quality and coherence. Not all these issues are of relevance to this study of skills. However, the paper did address issues of training and the quality of care. Although this consultation paper was issued under a different government, it seems that many of the general principles will continue to inform policy and the development of the National Childcare Strategy referred to above.

The development of National Training Organisations and sectoral targets

The development of National Training Organisations and sectoral training targets at the time of this research provided impetus to pressures for change already existing in the childcare sector. The 1996 DfEE consultation paper reports that a National Training Organisation for the childcare sector was being developed. This was likely to focus on training and education in childcare for those working with children up to the age of eight.

There was already strong pressure within the sector for the recognition of the importance of training for childcarers, and the more complete development of training opportunities. In 1992, a group of early years trainers and advisers started to meet at the National Children's Bureau to discuss the future of training for those work with young children. A number of concerns had led to these meetings. These included:

● concerns about the mismatch between the training needs of those working with young children and the opportunities available to them

● the lack of progress on developing NVQs in childcare and education, and

- concerns about changes in teacher training which impacted on early years teachers.

Subsequent interest in the education of young children and the introduction of the Government's nursery voucher scheme led to the reconvening of this group, as detailed by Pugh (1996). In 1993, the Early Childhood Education Forum (ECEF) was set up, bringing together 40 national organisations working with and for young children. This Forum is concerned with many aspects of provision, including policy, curriculum, training, inspection and funding. However, training has been an important area of consideration. In 1996, a review of developments and needs in training for work with young children was published by the Early Years Training Group of the ECEF (Pugh, 1996). This looks at what a strategy on training and qualifications might look like, and contributes to the agenda for change and recognition in this area. In particular, it is based on the premise:

> '. . . the years from birth to six years should be seen as a distinct phase, in which care and education are combined, and for which specialist training is required.' (Pugh, 1996)

The out-of-school childcare initiative

The out-of-school childcare initiative was introduced in 1993. It offers grant support to help with the start up costs of out-of-school childcare provision, whether this is before or after school, or during the holidays. The main aims of this initiative was to help parents and guardians of school age children participate more fully in the labour market, through improving the quantity and quality of out-of-school childcare. Since 1993, the success of the initiative in helping parents remain in or return to work has contributed to further government investment being put into the setting up of out-of-school clubs. There has been a vast expansion in out-of-school provision, which has brought new pressures to the need for skills in this sector. Working with school age children out of school hours requires some very different skills to working with pre-school age children. The expansion of this sector of childcare has, however, focused attention on the nature of these skill and the provision of training. This study focused on the skills needed for working with pre-school children, although Chapter 4 does briefly refer to this area of need.

Europe

The implications of being part of the EU did not emerge as a major issue in the course of this study, Nevertheless, membership does add to the on-going pressures for change in Britain. In March 1992, the Council of Ministers adopted a Recommendation on Child Care (DfEE, 1996). This committed each Member State to:

> 'Take and/or progressively encourage initiatives to enable women and men to reconcile their occupational, family and upbringing responsibilities arising from the care of children.'

The DfEE consultation document on childcare (DEE, 1996) goes on to detail some of the provisions available through the EU. For example, funds to support childcare are available through the European Structural Funds. The European Social Fund (ESF) can support vocational training in childcare and also pay for childcare costs if they are part of an ESF funded project design. These types of funding both contribute to the overall volume of provision, but also pressures for quality and training.

2.7 Conclusions

There is currently a great deal of debate amongst key actors in the sector, in particular about a firmer definition of the skills needed to work effectively with young children and the ways in which a greater proportion can become adequately qualified. In particular, there is considerable emphasis on childcare as a profession. The 'statement of underlying principles' for Early Years NVQs provides a clear and useful summary of the approach to childcare which is felt appropriate. The main headings under which these principles are summarised as:

- early years of life — the earliest years of children's lives are a unique stage of human development
- the welfare of the child
- working in partnership with parents/families
- children's learning and development
- equality of opportunity
- anti-discrimination
- keeping children safe
- confidentiality

- celebrating diversity
- working with other professionals
- the reflective practitioner.

There are many pressures for change within the childcare sector. Some of these pressures are external to the sector, occurring as a result of governmental priorities, and concerns and changes in society more generally, for example. Others are internal to the sector, as key actors work to improve the quality and physical infrastructure of care, alongside the provision of training and recognition of skills. What is perhaps interesting about this sector is that, although skill needs are changing, it is the recognition that caring for children does involve a body of skills and knowledge which has dominated recent years.

3. Working with the Elderly

3.1 Introduction

This chapter begins by presenting a general statistical picture of those employed in caring for elderly people. Using secondary sources, we briefly look at the size and composition of the occupation, employment status and pay levels. Elder care is delivered in different settings (*ie* in residential establishments, in clients' own homes and in day centres) according to clients' needs and circumstances. Using the findings from other studies, the second part of this chapter explores the nature of work, the type and level of care required in different settings, as well as the profile of the people who have traditionally worked in these areas.

A number of recent studies have shown how the demand for elder care has changed considerably in recent years, and is likely to change even further in the near future. The findings from the current investigation confirm these trends and highlight the implications for skill requirements in the occupation. The demographic, cultural and legislative changes which have influenced the type and level of elder care required are discussed in the final parts of the chapter. The findings on changes in the demand for elder care are based on our own research, as well as other recent relevant studies.

3.2 A statistical overview

3.2.1 Size and composition of the occupation

In 1996, there were nearly half a million people employed as 'care assistants or attendants', and they represented two per cent of the total workforce (LFS, 1996). The sector has grown considerably in the past five years, from just under 300,000 in 1991 to 447,350 in 1996 (LFS, 1996).

Care workers are much more likely to be employed in the public sector, mainly by local authority social services departments, compared with the workforce as a whole. Despite attempts to reduce the role of social services departments and to move towards a mixed economy of welfare, in 1996 40 per cent of care workers were employed by the public sector, compared to 27 per cent of the rest of the workforce. A high proportion of care workers were also working in the voluntary sector: ten per cent, compared with two per cent of workers in other occupations (LFS, 1996). This reflects the important role that charities and voluntary organisations have traditionally played in the delivery of social care and also, again, the shift towards a greater involvement of the independent sector in the delivery of care.[1]

Historically, this has been one of the most gender segregated occupations. In 1996, 92 per cent of care assistants were women, and this occupational group accounted for three per cent of all economically active women (LFS, 1996). The number of men employed as care workers has increased slightly over the past five years, from five per cent in 1991 to eight per cent in 1996 (LFS, 1991 and 1996). However, all indications are that this is likely to remain a highly feminised occupation for the foreseeable future.

Despite commonly held assumptions about this being an occupation for 'mature' people and, in particular, older women who wish to combine part-time employment with family responsibilities, the data in Table 3:1 show that the age composition of the occupation is similar to that of the workforce as a whole. The only exception is people in their 50s, who are

---

[1]   All the statistical data in this section refer to 'care assistants and attendants' as defined by the Standard Occupational Classification (SOC 644). This occupational group includes those working with adults with learning difficulties and disabilities, as well as those working with the elderly. It is not possible to obtain data for the whole occupation broken down by different client groups. However, information about care workers in the statutory sector shows that their composition (*eg* in terms of gender, age, employment status) does not vary significantly according to client group. Data on care staff in the statutory sector also show that the majority work with the elderly (LGMB/ADSS, 1993). So, although the statistical data included in this section covers a larger occupational group than the one investigated by the study, they present a fairly accurate picture in relation to its composition.

Table 3:1 Comparison of age composition of care workers and rest of the workforce, 1991 and 1996 (per cent)

Age group	Care workers		Other occupations	
	1991	1996	1991	1996
16-19	9	5	6	5
20-29	23	23	24	23
30-39	20	24	24	26
40-49	24	24	24	24
50-59	20	20	16	16
60-64	3	3	4	4
65 and over	1	1	2	2
Base (N =)	279,518	447,350	25,827,764	25,631,002

Source: LFS, 1991 and 1996

slightly over-represented. While the difference between the proportion of care workers in this age group and the rest of the workforce is small, it seems to have remained consistent over the years. The representation of different age groups has not changed significantly in the past five years, although there has been a small decrease in the proportion of 16 to 19 year olds. This probably reflects the growing trend during this period for young people to remain in full-time education.

3.2.2 Employment status and pay

Part-time working is widespread within the occupation. In 1996, nearly 60 per cent of female care workers were employed on a part-time basis, compared with 44 per cent of other women in employment. However, female care workers were slightly less likely to be in temporary employment than women in other occupations — five and eight per cent respectively (LFS, 1996).

The care sector workforce has traditionally been vertically segmented in terms of access to training, development and career opportunities. The top of the occupational hierarchy is highly skilled and trained, and positioned within a well defined career structure. At the bottom of the hierarchy, those in basic grade posts have very limited access to training and qualifications. They are often 'trapped' in very flat career structures offering few or no opportunities for development and promotion. These

Table 3:2 Average gross weekly earnings among different occupational groups, 1996

Occupational group	1996 weekly earnings £
All occupations, both sexes	352
Manual occupations, both sexes	281
Care workers, both sexes	182
Female care workers	177
Male care workers	209

Source: ONS, 1996

factors, combined with the high incidence of part-time work in the occupation, result in very low earning potentials.

Using data from the New Earnings Survey, Table 3:2 shows that this is one of the lowest paid occupations. In 1996, average weekly earnings for care workers were £182. This was nearly half the average earnings for the workforce as a whole (£352). It was also considerably lower than average earnings among other manual workers (£281) (ONS, 1996). Even within a low paid, predominantly female occupation, men tend to earn more than women. In 1996, the average weekly pay for male care workers was £209, compared to £177 for women. Furthermore, between 1991 and 1996, male care workers' pay grew at a slightly faster rate than that of their female counterparts — 13 per cent compared to 11 per cent.

3.3 Delivering care in different settings

The level and type of formal care required by elderly people varies considerably and depends on their physical and mental conditions, as well as the availability of informal care. Different types and levels of care are provided in different settings. Residential care is now considered appropriate only for very frail and dependent people requiring heavy care and support, while lesser levels of care can be provided in the community (*ie* at home and in day centres). The nature of the work, tasks and the skills required in different care settings are similar. However, some differences do exist, particularly in relation to the emphasis on different skills. In addition, career, training and development opportunities can vary considerably between different settings. The nature of work and tasks in different settings, and the characteristics of people who have traditionally worked in these areas, are explored below.

3.3.1 Residential care

Despite the move to care in the community, the majority of care staff are still employed in residential homes (see, for example, LGMB/ADSS, 1993). The independent sector plays an important part in the provision of residential care. Many of the largest voluntary organisations working with the elderly run residential homes. Private providers are also vital in meeting needs for residential care, particularly in some geographical areas (*ie* traditional retirement areas). The role of the independent sector in the provision of residential care is destined to grow even further, with an increasing number of local authorities likely to play a very marginal role, and increasingly concentrating on the provision of specialist residential care (*eg* rehabilitation centres, special units, respite care).

Traditionally the work of residential staff has focused on the provision of personal care (*eg* assisting clients with washing, bathing, dressing, *etc.*), with smaller homes also requiring workers to carry out domestic chores. However, there is now an increasing need for residential staff to provide medical care, and to play an active role in creating an environment where clients' emotional, psychological and social needs can also be met.

More than two-thirds of residential care staff work part time and the largest proportion are defined as manual workers (DHSSI, 1991). Like the occupation as a whole, residential work has been characterised by a lack of training and qualifications, low professional standards, and poor development and career opportunities. In 1967, the Williams Committee Report recommended the development of specialist training and career structures to attract staff with knowledge and skills to replace:

> '. . . the motherly woman, or the economical housekeeper, who have been the backbone of the service in the past.' (DHSSI, 1991, p.13)

More than 20 years later the findings and recommendations of the Wagner Committee (1988) showed that very little had changed:

> 'A commonly held view of care work is that it is unskilled and consists of little more than domestic chores. It is seen as particularly suitable for women, consistent with their traditional

roles in the home as carers. … Residential work, like other occupations in which women are predominant, is low paid, with low status, and poor conditions of service. Add to this the lack of training, adequate planning and support for staff, and it becomes clear that residential work does not yield such high expectations, as for instance, field social work. We believe that changes in the status, conditions and training support for staff are necessary to redress these imbalances.' (DHSSI, 1991, p.13)

In 1988, in recognition of the concern over the number of untrained staff in residential homes for the elderly, the Training Support Grant (TSG) was introduced. While the TSG has helped to boost vocational training, a recent study has shown that only a quarter of residential staff have a professional qualification, and just over half have some educational qualification — mainly GCSEs/'O' levels school leaving certificates (Balloch *et al.*, 1995).

3.3.2 Domiciliary care

While domiciliary care is provided to a range of clients (*eg* people with a disability or learning difficulty, and families with children at risk), this is mainly a service for the elderly, and 90 per cent of home care staff work with this client group (Balloch *et al.*, 1995). Domiciliary care is a relatively new service which has been growing steadily since the 1940s, and is destined to grow even further given the increased emphasis on community care. Traditionally domiciliary care has been provided mainly by local authorities, but the mixed economy of welfare has opened the door to a range of private providers. Voluntary organisations play a minor role in this area. They are, however, more likely to focus on respite care provided at home, where the emphasis is on personal and social care rather than domestic work. Unlike residential and nursing homes in the independent sector, private agencies providing domiciliary care do not have to register with the local authority and are not subject to inspections (*eg* from Social Services Inspector Units or the Health and Safety Executive).

In terms of personal characteristics and employment status, domiciliary workers are very similar to their colleagues in the residential sector. They constitute a large army of women who are low paid and work part time. Gender segregation is even more marked in this setting, with women making up 96 per cent of domiciliary staff, compared with 85 per cent in residential care. Home care staff are also more likely to work part time (73 per cent) compared with residential workers (31 per cent) (Balloch *et al.*, 1995).

Domiciliary care staff are the most scattered group of workers in the care sector with very little contact with their manager and colleagues. They have a high level of responsibility and freedom, but are also isolated and vulnerable. Individuals tend to develop their own ways of working in response to different clients' needs. With the move towards community care, they are increasingly expected to provide social care, as well as perform domestic duties (DHSSI, 1991).

Domiciliary care workers tend to have lower educational levels than residential staff. Only seven per cent of home care workers have a professional qualification, and just over one-third have some educational qualification. Again, these are mainly GCSEs/ 'O' levels or school leaving certificates (Balloch *et al.*, 1995).

In some ways domiciliary workers are considered to have even lower status than staff in residential homes. The *British Household Panel Study*, for example, classifies the former as unskilled manual and the latter as semi-skilled manual workers. Their status is negatively affected by the fact that they perform functions that might be otherwise provided by family members and in the same setting (*ie* in the home). Almost all domiciliary staff are graded as manual workers, and the fragmented nature of the service means that opportunities for training and development are even fewer in this setting than in residential care (Balloch *et al.*, 1995).

3.3.3 Day centres

Day centres for the elderly grew from voluntary social clubs in the 1950s, and now provide a range of activities and personal care. Many day centres are run by local authorities. However, voluntary organisations do play an important role in this area, while the private sector has traditionally had little involvement in this type of provision. The current emphasis on caring for elderly people in the community should stimulate the growth of day centres. However, in practice, because day centres provide preventative, non-statutory care, resources for this type of service are often among the first to be cut at times of financial restriction.

Day centre staff tend to acquire a detailed knowledge of the specific needs of their clients. In many cases they have to develop innovative ways of working, drawing on a wide range of skills and abilities. They have also been at the forefront of user participation initiatives.

Day centre staff working with the elderly represent a very small proportion of care workers and very little up-to-date information is available on this group. Again part-time work is widespread (two-thirds of the total), most are in the lower manual grades and around three-quarters are women. Only about one-sixth of those working in day centres for the elderly hold a qualification (DHSSI, 1991).

3.4 The changing demand for care

The nature and level of demand for care for the elderly has changed considerably in recent years, and this is leading to changes in skill requirements. A number of key factors have been influencing the demand for care for the elderly, including demographic changes, the increased participation of women in paid employment and high levels of geographical mobility among young people.

Demographic changes are resulting in a growing ageing population in Britain. Projections indicate that by the year 2001, the number of people aged 85 and over will have risen by 30 per cent, and by 2031 this could grow to 50 per cent (Corti and Dex, 1995). Not only is the quantity of care needed becoming greater because there are now more elderly people, but heavier and more complex care is also required (particularly in the residential sector). Elderly people live longer, and they are therefore more likely to be frail, suffering from dementia and a range of other medical conditions typical of old age.

Demographic changes are also affecting the numbers of middle age female relatives who have traditionally provided unpaid care for dependent, older people. A report on the future of care for the elderly in the European Union (McGlone and Cronin, 1994) showed that while in 1960 there were on average 2.4 women in the 45 to 69 age group for every person over 70, by 1990 this figure had fallen to just 1.6, and in some countries it is expected to reach a ratio of 1:1 in the near future.

The steady growth in women's participation in paid employment (and in particular older, married women) is also impinging on the demand for social care for the elderly. An increasing proportion of unpaid care which has traditionally been provided by this group of women in the private sector, will have to be provided in the public sector and be, at least partly, funded by the State (Corti *et al.*, 1994).

Finally, increasing migration has also diminished the care potential of the family in relation to the elderly. Younger generations are less likely to be living with or in proximity to elderly relatives (McGlone and Cronin, 1994).

3.5 Redefining the concept of care

In recent years, the way we think, talk about and conceptualise care has changed considerably, and this is leading to a change in the type, range and level of skills required in the occupation. Since the early 1980s, there has been an ongoing debate about how and where care should be delivered, whose needs and criteria should be considered in planning the delivery of care, and on issues around quality, cost-effectiveness and ensuring equality in service delivery.

The research findings reflect the growing importance of these issues which were explored in some depth with respondents. Organisational policies, practices and the very language used by interviewees in talking about their service delivery reflected a move away from what one research participant called:

> 'The warehouse model, where clients were treated like parcels and processed through the various stages of washing, dressing, feeding, etc.'

Common features of the 'warehouse' approach included the institutionalisation and routinisation of care, as service delivery was organised mainly around staff needs and the needs of units operating within large and inflexible bureaucracies. In the most extreme cases, this approach was dehumanising and led to mental and even physical abuse. However, even in less extreme circumstances, the tendency was to patronise elderly people and treat them like children, often denying them a level of independence, privacy and choice commensurate with their physical and mental abilities.

While in smaller, voluntary organisations the warehouse approach was perhaps less common, staff attitudes tended to be naive and unprofessional (*eg* 'do-gooders' who knew what was best for the clients). As a respondent in a voluntary organisation explained:

'When we started 15 years ago, we were very, very voluntary. We lacked policies, procedures, clear ideas about the type and quality of care we were aiming to provide, and the type of staff we needed to employ and develop. We saw it mainly as a quasi job done by ladies doing it for pin money.'

The shift in the care discourse is reflected by the range of themes and values which are increasingly influencing the planning and delivery of care. The themes and values emerging from the interviews can be summarised as follow:

- dignity
- rights
- empowerment
- choice
- fulfilment
- privacy.

Dignity

Dignity emerged as one of the most fundamental values, equally important across the different settings. It implies the recognition of the intrinsic value of people, regardless of circumstances, and it is put into practice by respecting individuals' uniqueness and personal needs. Dignity is closely linked to equal opportunities, and the idea that diversity (*eg* cultural, religious, ethnic, *etc.*) should be recognised, respected and valued. The need to emphasise this value is also linked to the stigma and loss of dignity often associated with mental health problems, physical disability and the need for assistance with intimate personal care. In residential homes, dignity is also about helping people to personalise their living space and their own room in particular.

Rights

Closely linked to dignity is the concept of rights associated with citizenship, such as freedom of expression, movement, conscience, and the right to choose, for example, whether to participate in care or treatment, or to establish personal and sexual relationships.

Empowerment

There has been a growing recognition that traditional attitudes towards elderly people, particularly if frail or confused, have tended to disempower them and take away their ability to act as independent human beings. Consequently, the concept of empowerment has become increasingly important. In practice, this is about ensuring that elderly people can 'achieve independence within dependence', and are given opportunities and encouraged to act independently, as far as is compatible with their own individual abilities.

Choice

The concept of empowerment presupposes that elderly people can exercise choice about the content of their daily lives. This means that whenever possible, clients should be able to choose from a range of options and have adequate information to make decisions. This value emerged as being particularly important in residential homes, where in the past institutionalisation and routinisation had tended to considerably reduce residents' ability to take even simple decisions about their everyday life (such as what clothes to wear, what food to eat, when to go out or have visitors).

Fulfilment

Fulfilment also emerged as another important value, and this was described in the values statement of one of the participating organisations as:

> 'The realisation of personal aspirations and abilities in all aspects of daily life.'

Fulfilment is realised by providing a stimulating environment and a range of physical (*eg* exercise sessions, outings) and intellectual activities (*eg* reminiscence and discussion groups, quiz games, reading sessions) aimed at developing clients' skills, abilities, interests and hobbies. Traditionally, one of the main aims of day centres has been to provide a range of intellectual and physical activities, but these are also becoming increasingly important in residential homes where clients have tended to lack stimulation and become very inactive.

Privacy

In the past, and particularly but not exclusively in residential homes, many elderly people were often denied the right to privacy. The emphasis on privacy emerged in several contexts and related to ensuring that:

- information about clients remains confidential
- clients can liaise with other people without intrusion or having to account for their actions
- the assistance required is kept to a minimum commensurate with clients' abilities
- clients receive personal care (*eg* bathing, using the toilet) without being overlooked or heard.

The research findings show that the emergence and growing importance of these values in the delivery of care are beginning to influence skill needs and requirements. This could lead to a greater professionalisation of the occupation and the establishment of higher entry requirements (*eg* in terms of competencies, experience and qualifications).

3.6 The wider context

The nature, type and quality of the care provided to the elderly has also been influenced by a range of other factors. The new care discourse, new ideas about how and where care should be delivered, and expectations about quality and minimum standards are reflected in recent legislative changes and government policy. The single piece of legislation which has had the most significant impact on the provision of elder care has been the National Health and Community Care Act (1990). However, other factors, outside the social policy framework, have also had an influence on recent developments in the care sector. These include more general ideas about accountability, quality and efficiency in the public sector. The development of occupational standards and competencies has encouraged many care providers to examine their skill requirements and training needs. Finally, recent health and safety legislation has also had a considerable impact on the care sector, and has led to a comprehensive review of practices and procedures in many areas of service delivery.

The 1989 White Paper *Caring for People* defines community care in terms of:

'. . . enabling people to live as normal life as possible, in their own homes and local communities.' (Secretary of State for Health *et al.*, 1989).

More specifically, the White Paper aimed to:

- promote the development of domiciliary, day and respite services to enable people to live in their own homes wherever feasible and sensible
- ensure that service providers make practical support for carers a high priority
- ensure that services are provided on the basis of proper needs assessment and good case management
- promote the growth of the independent sector alongside good quality public services in order to ensure greater diversity in provisions and a mixed economy of welfare
- clarify the responsibilities of agencies, ensure accountability for their performance, and monitor the quality of the care provided
- introduce a new funding structure in order to maximise efficiency and secure better value for money.

The principles of the White Paper were widely accepted in the care sector. Much of what was proposed was consistent with ideas about what constitutes good practice, and some of its elements had already been developed in the early 1980s in individual local authorities (Barnes and Wistow, 1992). However, community care has also been criticised for raising expectations about service provisions while failing to address the issue of how the steady increase in the demand for (good quality) social care can be met in the context of resource scarcity (*eg* Langan, 1990; La Valle and Lyons, 1996; Challis and Hugman, 1993).

A lack of resources and the sustained pressure to reduce unit costs have put care providers in all sectors in a very difficult position. On one hand they have to attract, retain and develop a more flexible, better skilled and better qualified workforce. On the other, the need to keep costs down means that resources for training and development are under pressure, and it is increasingly difficult to offer rewards commensurate with the greater responsibility and higher level work being required. As one respondent from a local authority explained:

'Because of tight unit costs and competition from the independent sector we need to avoid the pressure of pay increases,

while at the same time the job is being upgraded to meet statutory requirements and increasing clients' expectations.'

The growing tendency among employers to develop frameworks which define skill requirements and competencies in different occupations in line with organisational needs and clients' demands are beginning to influence the care sector as well. In some local authorities included in this study, reviews of skill needs in the occupation were being undertaken, competency frameworks for care staff were being developed, and skills scans and workforce analysis were being conducted to identify training needs.

Finally, health and safety legislation has had a considerable impact on the knowledge and skills that care workers are expected to have or acquire on the job. As discussed in Chapter 5, care workers must be aware of, and conform to, a range of health and safety procedures, and are expected to play an important role in identifying and reporting possible sources of risk.

3.7 Conclusion

Elder care is provided by a large army of part-time female workers. The occupation has traditionally been characterised by low pay, part-time work, poor development, training and career opportunities. The low status of the occupation is clearly linked to low entry requirements and, until recently, the lack of widely recognised occupational standards and qualifications. However, the research findings show that a number of factors might lead to a greater professionalisation of the occupation and enhance its status. A growing demand for more complex care requires a wider range of high level skills. A number of cultural and legislative changes are also influencing the provision of care with clearly established values, criteria, policies and procedures now more likely to influence service delivery. While these changes require a better skilled workforce, our respondents did express concern about the lack of resources to upskill care workers and to offer them rewards commensurate with the increasing demands of the job.

4. Skills for Childcare

4.1 Introduction

Our literature search found relatively few studies specifically addressing the skills needed to care for pre-school age children. There are references to the importance of skilled workers. For example, a Kent Childcare Network document comments:

> 'The quality of any playgroup is ultimately dependent upon the skills, attributes and commitment of the adults who work in them.'

The undervaluing of the skills needed to work with children was also emphasised. The association between perceptions of what is skilled work and the extent to which an occupation is dominated by women was discussed earlier. However, other studies have raised a number of other issues which contribute to the perception that childcare is a relatively low-skilled occupation. For example, Holland (1995) challenges several myths surrounding childcare, and in particular the arguments that: 'childcare comes naturally to women', and 'childcare isn't really skilled, it is babysitting'. Holland reports that these types of arguments have led to the assumption that:

> 'If childcare comes naturally, childcare workers do not need training, they do not need supervision and the argument follows that they barely need paying for something so natural.'

She goes on to argue that childcare work is physically and mentally demanding, involving many different kinds of communication and managerial skills:

> 'It is not a lack of skills involved; it is the wholesale undervaluing of these skills.'

It is, however, apparent that the skills needed to work in childcare are of growing interest and concern, not least with the development of NVQs, concerns about the safety of children, pressures from Europe, and as consideration is given to the establishment of a National Training Organisation in childcare and education. In 1988, Cohen noted an increased degree of professionalism in playgroups. In 1990, the report of the Rumbold Committee into the quality of the educational experience offered to three and four year olds (DES, 1990) argued that those working with these age groups need a range of skills and attributes to assure a high quality experience for children. They identified a number of skill areas thought to be central to this area of childcare:

- the development of particular skills, interest and expertise in a subject or curriculum area, and awareness of appropriate strategies for work with young people
- skill in implementing and planning the curriculum in order to ensure breadth, balance and continuity with the national curriculum
- organisational skills and strategies for effective learning
- observational skills and effective monitoring, recording and assessment of the curriculum
- interactive and communication skills
- management and leadership skills
- skills in collaborative working, including working with parents and other professionals
- skill and ability to provide, or facilitate the provision of, equal opportunities for all under fives, notwithstanding differences of race, gender and educational need.

Our findings, although based on a small number of interviews, suggest that childcare workers do require a wide range of abilities, knowledge and skills. It is not simply a matter of making sure the children under their care are safe, but of having a far greater depth of understanding about children and how they behave, learn and play, for example. A very recent report (Pugh, 1996) concludes:

> 'The education and care of young children is a complex and demanding job that requires a highly skilled and well-trained workforce.'

This chapter discusses the skills reported to be needed of childcare workers, using the term 'skill' in its broadest sense. The sample on which these findings are based was small and covered a range of different types of provision. There were some variations in the expectations placed on childcare workers working in different environments and at different levels of seniority. However, there were also many similarities. We spoke to a range of different types of respondent, not all of whom were employers. Many were working to promote the training and development of people working with young children, and very much emphasising current 'good practice'. Our findings on skill needs are, therefore, possibly verging towards the ideal and best practice, and at times comment is made about the range of approaches in practice.

A key aim of this research is to explore how skill needs are changing within occupations. It is very difficult to discuss current skill needs in isolation from change, and the following sections frequently refer to current and evolving needs. A separate section at the end of this chapter does, however, identify the main ways in which skill needs are changing.

4.2 Basic skills

Working with children, including very young children, does require a basic level of literacy and numeracy. This might seem an obvious statement. However, as emphasis is placed on pre-school childcare being about learning and development, these types of skills assume greater importance. One manager reported having some difficulties recruiting staff who had sound literacy skills:

> 'Every child should be exposed to reasonably good English and spelling. You sometimes see displays with spelling mistakes and it's not setting a good example.'

A lack of confidence with maths and science among those working with pre-school children was another concern. Many people entering childcare have little, if any, confidence in using numbers and in basic mathematics and science, and may even feel inhibited by the subject. Managers and others we interviewed commented on the importance of not passing this inhibition on to the children. Pre-school experience provides the basic building blocks on which children's future mathematical and scientific knowledge is based, and it is important that these are firmly in place.

There are other reasons why literacy, in particular — including grammar, spelling and being able to speak reasonably — are important. Providers of childcare need to keep records of a child's progress, for example, and any special needs they might have. The former of these is becoming more widespread as greater attention is paid to the learning and development of young children, and with the advent of Nursery Education Vouchers.[1] The Children's Act established the Key Worker system. Each worker is responsible for a group of children, and must ensure that the needs of their group are met. They are also required to record activities and progress, and this information is sent home for parents to see and comment on. Accurate, legible and intelligible recording is essential. In addition, long hours of care and the provision of appropriate learning activities, for example, require careful planning and team working. These also involve written and oral recording, and communication.

4.3 Personal skills and attributes

A wide range of personal skills and attributes were reported to be of importance. These included:

- good communication skills
- the ability to work as an effective and reliable team member
- being reliable, committed, enthusiastic
- being organised and a good planner
- punctuality
- maturity and experience
- taking initiative and able to cope with responsibility
- being assertive
- having patience
- flexibility — being able to deal with the unexpected and the unknown
- coping with change, including taking responsibility for one's own learning
- personal appearance — 'Must be well presented. It is about appropriateness, wearing appropriate clothes.'

Some of the characteristics listed above are very much personal attributes, others can more fully be described as personal skills.

---

[1]   Although these are now being withdrawn, the desirable learning outcomes were still in place at the time of writing this report.

A similar list to this appears among the requirements for many jobs. However, the context in which they are applied varies. This is an important aspect of employers' skill needs, and emerges as a constant theme throughout this whole programme of research. This section discusses the particular application of some of these attributes and skills in jobs caring for young children.

Looking after children was frequently reported to be:

> '. . . emotionally and physically demanding.'

Carers need to be able to cope with these demands. They need to be patient, assertive and flexible in their dealings with children and parents.

Interpersonal skills were reported to be very important and, indeed, they underlie many of the other, more job specific skills required of childcare workers. Carers need to be able to communicate with colleagues, children, parents, and possibly other professionals. Not all childcare workers will be required to work with or relate to all these groups, but at a minimum they will need to be able to relate to colleagues and children. However, whoever they are communicating with, the expectation will be that they will deal with these people appropriately.

It was expected that children should be treated as individuals and not spoken down to:

> 'What is important is to treat children as individuals. . . . Skilled workers treat each child individually, but there are a lot of childcarers who haven't thought of this.'

Although children might not have the level of understanding of adults, it was argued that this does not mean that they should be spoken to in a condescending or too simplistic a manner. Different personalities and approaches are often needed, depending on the age of the children being looked after. For example, it was reported that those working in the baby room had to be:

> '. . . calm, quiet, softly spoken, have a softer nature. They must be able to communicate with the babies, and stimulate them. Babies are probably the hardest to work with because they have to do all of the inputting and don't get anything back. For some people this is really hard because they have to keeping it going.'

Those working with toddlers need different types of understanding:

> 'With the toddlers you need extreme patience because of
> tantrums and frustrations with this age group.'

Fitting in and working in a team received particular emphasis,
and many of the other interpersonal skills mentioned also relate
to this:

> 'Ability to work as an effective and reliable team member. I think
> that's very important because a team functions as a whole. . . .
> what each one of those team members brings is skills to
> complement that whole.'

Within a playgroup or a nursery, for example, staff do not work
in isolation. There should always be several carers present and
they need to be able to work together effectively, sharing information and concerns. This does not mean that all the staff need
to have the same strengths. In a number of interviews, the
scheme manager talked about their staff having complementary
strengths and weaknesses. For example, one scheme manager
reported that some of her staff were better at discipline than
others, while others were extremely well organised and could
always spot what had been missed. Another reported how
various members of staff could relate to different groups of
children more easily than others. What was important was having
a balance, so that all needs and personalities could be catered for.

Taking initiative and being responsible were other areas which
received emphasis. These traits tend to develop with maturity
and experience. However, a number of childcare workers,
particularly those working as a nanny for example, find they
have heavy levels of responsibility very early in their careers. In
many ways, there is a need for a common sense approach, and
for people to be able to deal with emergencies and difficult
situations calmly and appropriately.

Taking responsibility has broader implications, which also relate
to flexibility. Staff in nurseries and playgroups, for example,
may have to take over a range of responsibilities, sometimes at
short notice. Unlike in some businesses, if a member of staff is
unwell or away, it might not be possible to leave their tasks for
another day. The children still have to be cared for, and the
usual activities covered. Furthermore, managers reported that

looking after children is a job which can rarely be restricted to 'office hours':

'It's not just a question of walking in at nine o'clock, getting the equipment out, playing with the children, and then clearing up and going home. It's taking home their bits with them and, for example, the evaluations.'

Respondents also talked about having to deal with conflict and problems as they arose, diffusing situations of conflict, and avoiding the development of aggressive situations. These situations might involve the children themselves, parents or others involved in the provision of care. Although in many situations a supervisor, or experienced member of staff would be involved, this is not always the case. All carers, therefore, need to be aware of the possibility of such situations arising, what might trigger them, and how to deal with and diffuse them:

'. . . dealing with conflict in different situations. For example, dealing with conflict such as children in conflict with each other, dealing with parents and dealing with other colleagues.'

'Managing conflict time and again comes up across the board. It's a problem and sometimes things like bullying, racism and equality come up.'

Coping with change and continuing learning were raised as related issues. It was reported that childcare is a rapidly changing area. The understanding of child behaviour and development, and ideas about the most appropriate approaches for example, have evolved considerably in recent years and continue to do. There is also much more legislation, and regulation surrounding the provision of childcare. Carers, therefore, need to be able to cope with these changes and their implications. They also need to keep their own skills and knowledge up to date:

'Someone who is willing and able to train. This is a problem. There are nursery nurses who have been stuck in their jobs for 20 years and have had no access to training.'

An issue related to taking responsibility is the need for many childcare workers to be aware of their own rights and the boundaries within which they operate. It was reported that many managers, especially those running small, private nurseries and playgroups, and parents employing childcarers directly, for example, are not fully aware of their responsibilities as an employer, or of employee rights. Although not truly a skill, it is advisable for people working as childcarers to be aware of their rights as an employee.

A further issue raised was the need for childcarers to be aware of the necessity of working within certain boundaries, for example through reporting and recording accidents, and particular incidents of bad behaviour. If anything does go wrong it is important that scheme managers and parents are aware of what happened, the circumstances, and subsequent actions. These types of boundaries are set to protect both the children and their carers, and it is important that this is understood. One respondent reported that the boundaries within which carers work are:

> '. . . getting narrower and narrower and narrower all the time.'

Relating to parents

Communicating and dealing with parents was not seen to be the responsibility of all staff in some types of provision. However, in many circumstances, childcare workers will have to deal directly with parents. It was reported that in some provision, only carers at a certain level of seniority were supposed to deal with parents. This was seen as unsatisfactory by many. The NVQ, for example, requires some contact with parents, and it was generally accepted that all those involved in providing care should be able to relate to parents and other carers.

A wide range of issues were raised in relation to this area. Overall, there is a need for an awareness of the feelings of parents, their perspective and situation. One respondent commented:

> 'A lot of parents need a lot of reassurance, they are angry and guilty because they are going out to work. There may also be conflicts between partners as to whether children should be in daycare.'

At a minimum, a childcarer might be expected to be aware of and sensitive to these feelings. In other circumstances they might be expected to work with the parents, discussing how they feel and helping them to come to terms with their feelings. One area of potential difficulty raised was the need to help children and parents prepare for school. This illustrates a need for carers to be able to deal with conflict and mediate between different ideas of what is appropriate:

> 'Helping parents to prepare their children for school is important. This is sometimes a euphemism for telling parents they should help their child to act more appropriately for school. This can be difficult because the parent may take offence and take the child out of the nursery, so childcarers must be mature enough to handle these situations. It is useful to have a mixed age range of staff and some with children themselves or who worked as nannies, etc. so they understand the full dynamics of families.'

Childcarers who live with the family — usually nannies, but also au pairs for example — need to be particularly aware of these types of issue and the dynamics within a family. A great deal of sensitivity is needed in these circumstances. Having another person living in a household, who is closely involved with the family can create many pressures and tensions which the carer (as well as others in the household) has to be aware of, able to understand and deal with. This takes considerable maturity and personality.

Some general examples were given in the course of our interviews. A woman who has recently had a baby and is just returning to work for example, is likely to be feeling a variety of emotions related to her recent pregnancy and how she looks physically, returning to work after a gap, and leaving her child for the first time. She might feel threatened and uneasy about having a young woman living closely with her family. In addition, carers in this type of situation will need to be aware of parental reactions more generally. Equally, very few people are even-tempered all the time. Living as part of a household, a nanny will need to understand, for example, that a parent being rude to them might be a consequence of the kind of day they have had and other things going on within that household, rather than specific personal antipathy towards the carer. Other possible areas of conflict which might arise include the range of activities the carer is responsible for, and how the children are looked after.

Overall, carers who live in need the strength of personality, and possibly an external network of support, to deal with a wide range of circumstances. They need a broader knowledge than that related just to dealing with and looking after children. They need to understand more generally about human behaviour, and how to approach and deal with potential conflict situations. Negotiating and influencing skills enter into this.

Another group, childminders, are likely to experience a different dynamic with parents. They are looking after children in their own homes, and have to be aware of how parents might feel about leaving their child in such an environment. Childminders are also running their own business and need to be able to be firm with parents about the conditions under which they operate, for example: what their fees are; what happens about paying if the child is ill, or on holiday or not able to attend; 'rules' around the circumstances under which it is acceptable to pick their child up late. There might be other areas where there is scope for negotiation between parents and a childminder, but ground rules for the relationship need to be set.

An important area of interaction between parents and childcare workers is likely to be over how a child is behaving and generally doing, and the type of care provided. Approaches to childcare have varied over time and parents might not always agree with the type of care being provided. For example, there is now a greater emphasis on child centred learning, allowing children to discover and create things themselves. This might not lead to the nicely written and coloured outputs which some parents think should be decorating classroom walls. It is likely that parents will find the type of childcare provision which most closely fits with their views of how children should be brought up. However, there is not always a choice and this is likely to be an issue over which there will be some discussion and negotiation. Carers might also need to be able to discuss concerns about a child's behaviour or their general progress, again issues which often need a degree of sensitivity in approach. Overall, it was reported that ideally some sort of partnership needs to develop between carers and parents so that both are in broad agreement and working together in contributing to a child's development.

4.4 Physically caring for children

Although there is much more to caring for children than making sure they are physically safe, this is still an important role. Childcare workers need to have knowledge of health and safety, fire regulations and child protection issues. They need to know what makes an environment safe for children. Concern about child abduction and other dangers means that staff also have to be aware of who should be around, who is around, and be prepared to challenge strangers. A recent evaluation of out-of-school provision in one locality found that safety is of increasing concern to parents and plays an important role in their choice of club (Giles *et al.*, 1996).

The type of caring provided and the levels of care needed will also depend on the age of the children being looked after. Staff working in a baby room or caring for very young children elsewhere need to provide different levels of care compared to those working with toddlers and immediate pre-school age children. It is often assumed that these types of skill and know-ledge are intuitive or common sense, especially among women, but this is not necessarily the case. People looking after children need to be consciously aware of how children's needs vary by, for example, age.

Understanding children's health and first aid are other areas of knowledge and expertise needed by those working with children. They need to be able to cope with accidents and any immediate first aid needs, whether relatively minor or serious in nature. They also need to be able to identify possible problems, be able to cope with children with various health conditions and who need regular treatment of some kind.

A number of other areas of knowledge were mentioned which broadly fall under this heading. These include: knowledge of child protection legislation (and what to do if there appears to be a problem, or a child confides in a carer), basic hygiene, nutrition, and child nutrition in particular.

A related area of skill and knowledge was the need for those looking after children to be able to look after themselves. Many activities involved in looking after children can be physically demanding. For example, lifting young children can place a strain on backs, and kneeling on knees. There are right and wrong ways of doing these things. One respondent commented:

> *'Many childcarers get bad backs and bad knees but it's not recognised in childcare.'*

4.5 A liking for working with children

Many studies of the career aspirations of school leavers have found that young women report a desire to work with children. Although some have stronger career aspirations, many see caring for children as a nice thing to do, something they can do, for example. However, simply wanting to look after children is rarely enough. Those working in childcare need:

'. . . a natural feeling for children, [someone] who can sit down and play with them, whether it is in the sandpit or something.'

'. . . a general empathy, a love of children.'

One respondent commented:

'There are no innate abilities which make somebody a good childcarer. If you start talking about innateness and personal attributes you get into stereotypes of motherliness etc., and you end up with childcarers who are doing it for all the wrong reasons.'

Although not truly a skill, people working with children need to be truly motivated and committed to the work. It is also increasingly expected that they will have thought out why they want to work in the area, and it is likely that these motivations will be explored in a job interview. Another respondent reported that they look for what has triggered people to want to work with children:

'We are looking for positive reasons. In very crude terms, we exclude people with a personality defect. We are not looking for people who lost out in their childhood and want to make up for this in providing care.'

4.6 Understanding and managing child behaviour

One important area of knowledge and skill for working with children is an understanding of child behaviour and how to manage this:

'Communication is important. It is partly about being intuitive and partly about good observation, watching children, what they like to do, what they avoid; identifying ways to help children recognise their individuality. There is a lot of talk in education circles to do with being child-centred and child-directed, but getting people to understand what it means is difficult. There are

lots of academics talking about it but it's still not getting through to childcarers and parents.'

There are a range of different approaches to managing child behaviour and over time views about what is and what is not acceptable have changed and evolved. There seems to be a general consensus that the most appropriate approach is to reinforce positive behaviours rather than punish negative behaviours. Not all nurseries, playgroups and child carers adopt these approaches; our sample tended to include providers who had given more conscious thought to skill and training needs. Nevertheless, those involved in developing training programmes and qualifications, for example, emphasise the need for those looking after children to understand the various approaches to managing behaviour, the advantages and disadvantages of each, and how ideas are evolving.

It is widely accepted that children should not be smacked or physically punished in any way while they are the responsibility of a non-family member. Indeed, local authorities do not allow childminders to smack children under their care. There is an emphasis on reinforcing positive behaviour through encouraging children in these areas. Children behaving negatively or 'badly' should be distracted, and persuaded to do something else or act differently, rather than just being told to 'stop it' or 'behave yourself'. There is also a greater emphasis on the capacity of children to understand so that, where appropriate, it should be explained why certain actions are or are not acceptable:

> *'If you don't treat [children] as individuals and understand their emotional make-up, you can't help them to cope with their frustrations or anxieties, and lots of children's poor behaviour later on in school is because nobody helped them to understand themselves. Treat them as individual and you can help redirect them and understand them.'*

In some circumstances, understanding child behaviour and recognising the causes of poor behaviour are key for other reasons. Poor or erratic behaviour might be a sign that a child is being abused or is medically hyperactive. In a nursery or playgroup, responsibility for identifying and acting on these types of behaviour will lie with a group and less experienced staff will be able to draw on the knowledge of other staff. Childminders and nannies, for example, will need the confidence to discuss any concerns with other professionals.

4.7 Knowledge and understanding of child development

As with managing child behaviour, there are a range of different approaches to child development. The theoretical understanding and underpinning knowledge of how children develop has progressed over time and alongside this, there have been changes in the approach to managing child development. People working with children need to understand current thinking, the reasons behind this and how this converts into practice.

Pugh (1996) provides a useful summary of the aspects of child development which people involved with young children need to understand. This goes into greater depth than our data, and illustrates the complexity of the knowledge needed:

- 'the processes of how children learn, and their developing ways of thinking and reasoning'
- 'how their language is acquired, and its development promoted or hindered'
- 'how they learn to develop their creative and innovative abilities'
- 'how they begin to acquire concepts in maths, science, history, geography'
- 'the ways in which they build up their personal concepts of self, of morality and acceptable social behaviour'
- 'the kinds of experiences they need to develop their physical skills'
- 'the crucial role of play as a major determinant of all this learning'.

The early years are a crucial time for socialisation and setting the grounding for a child's future development and adaptation within society generally. People working with pre-school children therefore play a major role, and need to understand how they can facilitate, or indeed hinder, the development of children under their care. An area which was commented on most frequently during our interviews was the importance of learning through play, of drawing out learning experiences from different activities and making learning fun. At the same time, it is important that the intrinsic value of play itself is not lost sight of. This point is also made by Pugh (1996):

> 'Educators need to remember that whilst children themselves modify their play as they grow older, it's intrinsic qualities

remain, making it important that practitioners continue to endorse it "as a legitimate mode of working within the classroom".'

It was reported that people working with children must be able to help children draw meaning and understanding out of activities. Children need adult input to help create meaning and understanding and to learn. This puts considerable responsibility on childcarers. They often need to be creative and proactive in identifying opportunities to help children in these ways. They also need to have knowledge of the stages of development children go through, and make their input at the right level for an individual. The difficulties some adults have in providing this type of input was commented on:

'They tend to see play as a child's world, which adults should not enter.'

Many examples were given of how learning opportunities can be created, and these were not confined to a nursery or playgroup environment. Childminders and nannies might involve children in domestic activities, both in the home and outside, including visits to shops or a library. Sorting laundry might include counting, matching colours, for example.

The introduction of Nursery Education Vouchers, and their associated learning outcomes was, at the time of our interviews, leading to an increased emphasis on the educational content of pre-school childcare. Although the vouchers have now been withdrawn, there is a continued emphasis on this educational content. All providers will need to show they can provide the relevant educational activities for four year olds. This will not just be left to those providers who see early education as important. An emphasis on education did not always seem to be new, but what is different is the more explicit emphasis on the educational content of pre-school childcare:

'Good people in childcare have always been doing the education thing but don't recognise it in themselves. They were doing it from a different perspective from education. It has been helpful to childcarers to recognise that the good practice has been doing the education all along.'

The importance of good basic skills was discussed above. However, one consequence of the greater emphasis on the role of pre-school childcare in child development and education is a greater emphasis on the intellectual ability of people working with young children. They need a basic understanding of a range of different subjects if they are to help children develop and learn through and across a range of activities.

4.8 Administration and observation

Partly as a consequence of the Children Act and the introduction of Nursery Education Vouchers (at the time of this study), but also due to more general changes in approach to childcare, there is a much greater requirement to observe and record children's progress. A number of childcare providers do maintain records of all the children under their care; these might comment generally on progress and behaviour. It is also important that any difficulties are noted as well as the outcomes of discussions with parents. In a nursery or group provision, this also contributes to some sort of continuity of care with staff changes. The growing emphasis on the educational content of pre-school childcare, especially for four year olds, means that records are often kept of learning outcomes for each child. These types of activity mean that many people working with children need good observational skills and to be able to record these in a clear and straightforward manner.

4.9 Equal opportunities

A key area of knowledge and understanding needed by workers in childcare is around equal opportunities. This is a term which is frequently used and often little understood. People looking after children need a full understanding of what equal opportunities means, and how to operationalise the concept in practice. For example, they need to understand that different children and their parents have varying needs and these, as far as possible, have to be addressed and met. Equal opportunities does not mean that every child should be treated alike, but that everyone should be provided with the circumstances and opportunities they personally need to progress and develop. One respondent discussed this issue in particular depth:

> 'It's very rare that someone will sit where you're sitting and say "right, to me equal opportunities means recognising the individual for what they are". I detest it when people say that they will treat people the same and a lot of people say "oh, I've got a lot of black friends" or just waffle on about the race issue and forget gender equality. Disability doesn't even come into the picture.'

Understanding the needs and position for children from different ethnic backgrounds, with disabilities and learning difficulties is important.

Inner city providers in particular reported concerns about the knowledge needed of staff catering for the needs of a mix of different races and cultures. It is not simply a matter of understanding that racism and bullying of other children because they are different is inappropriate. Childcarers need the knowledge and experience to deal with difficult situations if they arise, and to be able to defuse potentially difficult situations before anything happens. In addition, different cultures may vary in their approach and attitudes, for example, to discipline and managing child behaviour. These differences need to be understood and taken into account, and may require some negotiation and discussion with parents about what is and what is not acceptable, from the point of view of both carer and family.

Another area of expertise mentioned specifically in this study was providing appropriate care and support for children with special needs, in particular those with a disability or learning difficulty. Many providers rarely have to deal with children with special needs, and therefore having the precise skills and abilities among their staff may not be seen as important. Nevertheless, a general understanding of the particular needs of these children is useful. Some managers reported that they had staff specially trained in, for example, sign language.

4.10 Out-of-school childcare

The majority of our interviews were with providers of pre-school childcare. There has been a recent growth in provision of out-of-school childcare. Some of the skills and knowledge are the same as those needed by people working with pre-school children. However, out-of-school care does raise a number of other issues, not least because an older age range of children is being catered for. Children aged between five and 12 attend out-of-school clubs. In addition, the care is being provided at a time when these children would normally expect to be away from a school and formal learning environment.

Examples of the particular areas of expertise and knowledge required of people providing out of school childcare include:

- awareness of the different needs of children after (or possibly before) a day at school — some children want to relax, others want to do their homework, while others might want to join in a range of activities. Indeed, the current focus on homework could mean that in the future there will be a greater emphasis on the ability of those working in out-of-school clubs to help with homework.

- there are different views about the extent to which out-of-school care should be aiming to be developmental and learning

- the emotional, psychological and social needs of children between the ages of five and 11, and possibly 16, vary considerably.

Out-of-school childcare does introduce a different emphasis, compared to pre-school care, on the abilities of carers in sports, arts and crafts, and play more generally. Sport and other active activities, and arts and crafts are popular with those attending out-of-school clubs (see for example, O'Brien and Dench, 1996 and Dench and O'Regan, 1998). Staff therefore need to have abilities in these areas. One respondent did, however, comment:

> 'It's not necessarily about being good at any [of these activities], it's about having a go at doing them.'

4.11 Managerial and business skills

There is little career structure available for those working with pre-school children. In larger organisations there are some opportunities for promotion. Many childcarers who stay in the occupation eventually set up their own business. Supervisory and managerial positions require a range of staff and business management skills and knowledge. These will include financial, budgetary and business planning skills, as well as knowledge of employment law, employee rights, and recruitment procedures, for example. Anyone setting up as childminder will also require a range of skills around managing a business, although they are unlikely to have any staff.

These skills are rarely important early in a person's career. However, the basis often needs to be established then. This is an area of skill need which has largely been ignored, although increasingly it is being built into the training of those running out-of-school clubs in some areas, for example.

4.12 Changing skill needs

This chapter has focused on current skill needs, although reference has frequently been made to how these are changing and evolving. Other studies have concluded that the skills needed to provide childcare are undervalued and that it is a challenging and skilful job. This study also suggests that although childcare has always required a high level of ability and knowledge, greater thought and recognition is now being given to what it actually takes to provide good quality childcare. Emphasis is being placed on childcarers needing to have a body of recognised skill and knowledge. Indeed, many of our respondents talked about the 'professionalisation' of childcare:

> 'There are no innate abilities which make somebody a good childcarer. It's about learned skills, and training needs to be well planned and well resourced. We would like to see it being given a higher status at school level. We are talking about people responsible for future citizens and it is incredibly important that the job should be given more value.'

At the forum discussing the findings of this study there was some debate about the extent to which skills needs in childcare were really changing. Some experts felt that it was not so much that the actual skills required were changing, but rather that the world has changed:

> 'The skills haven't changed but the potential for damage to children has changed.'

> 'Children haven't changed but the world has and responsibility for preparing children for life has increased. We need to give children the skills to deal with a rapidly changing world. This requires different roles and understanding.'

There can, however, be no doubt that the role and job of a childcarer is changing. Those looking after pre-school children now have greater responsibilities than in the past, as life in general has become more complex and child safety, for example, has become a prime concern. There is more scope to use the theoretical knowledge underlying childcare. One respondent ended their interview with the following summary:

> 'There have been many changes in the childcare field. They have moved from providing the safe, warm environment to providing the under-fives curriculum. Childcare is much more formalised.

There is also the issue of childcare moving more into the counselling side, for example with involvement with the parents.'

Emphasis is increasingly being placed on the impact of early education and socialisation on experience in later life, especially as research can now be quoted which illustrates this. Although still important, providing a safe environment and catering for the basic needs of children is seen as a given rather than the prime focus. Ideally, people working with children need increasingly to understand child behaviour and development and how these can be managed. They need to be innovative and creative, take responsibility and initiative. Communication skills are very important, and relationships with both children and parents need to be developed.

Perhaps the biggest changes in recent years have been as a consequence of the Children Act and moves to increase the educational content of the pre-school curriculum. Literacy and numeracy in particular, but also other basic educational know-ledge and abilities are increasingly important. Furthermore, carers are now expected to observe and record information about the children under their care. It is amazing that these basic skills have not always been important, but our evidence suggests that this is the case:

'There continue to be too many lower level candidates and these are being allowed in.'

Carers now need a higher level of educational ability and basic skills than in the past.

One respondent summarised the requirements of a good nursery nurse as including the following:

'Child-centredness; good knowledge and understanding of child behaviour and how to manage it; general empathy with and love of children; up-to-date knowledge and understanding of children's learning and of health; the ability to observe accurately and report observations; up to date knowledge and basic understanding of child protection and policies; a general understanding of equal opportunity issues; and recognising positive self-esteem.'

In many respects our interviews focused on the 'ideal' and 'best practice'. One respondent reported being horrified by what she had seen when visiting certain day nurseries. For example, some organisations rely very much on relatively immature, inexperienced and untrained staff, who are often unsupervised and regularly work long hours. There was much talk among the people we interviewed about the 'professionalisation' of child-care, and there are many pressures for change in the sector. Part of the change has been a greater emphasis on the skills actually needed to work with children. However, it is also clear that requirements are changing. Furthermore, many of the skills required are based on an evolving body of knowledge and information, for example in relation to child behaviour and development, health and protection. It is not enough to learn one set of knowledge for life. Those working with children, as in so many other occupations, need to be prepared to keep their skills and knowledge up to date:

> 'Knowledge about child development has deepened over the last few years. People need greater knowledge and the theoretical framework.'

5. Skills for Eldercare

5.1 Introduction

Generally speaking, the occupational structure for care staff working with the elderly includes three broad levels (*ie* basic level staff, senior care workers and managers) requiring people with a different range of skills and at the different levels. However, the research findings show occupational and career structures can vary considerably according to setting, sector and employer size. The study included small (*ie* less than 50 staff) private and voluntary organisations with very flat career structures, with all care staff appointed at the same level and no internal opportunities for promotion and career development. At the other extreme, local authorities and many of the larger (*ie* over 250 staff) independent providers have well defined career structures, often with four or five levels separating basic level posts from management positions, and offering staff (albeit a limited number) sufficient training and development opportunities to move up the career ladder. Almost all the larger organisations could offer examples of managers who had worked their way up the career ladder after starting in basic level posts as care workers or even cleaners.

In this chapter, the nature of work, tasks, educational and skill requirements at each level are explored. The chapter focuses on basic level and senior care workers, while the discussion on skill requirements for management positions will be brief. Some of the requirements at the management level are specific to the care sector. However, most of the skills expected reflect management skills in general, and are therefore outside the remit of this study.

5.2 Basic level care workers

The research findings show that the nature of work and the tasks performed by basic level care workers are almost exclusively related to the direct provision of care. Examples of summaries of job descriptions for workers at this level are presented below:

'The purpose of this position is (1) to share with other staff in meeting the personal care needs of residents in a way that respects the dignity of the individual and promotes independence; (2) to share in the care of the residents' physical environment and in the general day-to-day activities of the Home.' (Job description for residential care worker in a large voluntary organisation)

'The purpose of the job is to give practical help, care and support to clients who need assistance in their own homes. The service promotes the continued independence of the client in the community. Services may be provided for people living alone or with other family members. The job involves carrying out personal and caring tasks that are not the responsibility of a nurse but which could normally be undertaken by a member of the client's family.' (Job description for domiciliary care worker in a local authority)

The research findings show that relevant experience is normally required for these positions. However, unpaid experience (for example, looking after a family, or voluntary work) is generally regarded as sufficient. 'Life experience' and 'maturity' were mentioned as being as important and equally valued as an 'x' number of years spent in a relevant paid job.

The research findings also show that in all settings, educational and relevant professional qualifications are not required. In some larger organisations (and particularly in local authorities) NVQ programmes are being set up and staff at this level are encouraged to work towards NVQ Level 2. In some organisations, NVQ Level 2, or the equivalent City and Guilds qualification in social care, are seen as desirable. However, all interviewees believed that it would be unrealistic to expect new recruits to have relevant qualifications, given that historically this has been an unqualified workforce, and there has been no comprehensive and systematic attempt to train care workers to widely recognised standards. Some respondents predicted that (resources permitting) the current move towards a more systematic approach to the identification of skill requirements and training needs in the occupation might result in NVQ Level 2 becoming a more common requirement for basic level care posts.

The sample included organisations where care workers could only be appointed at a basic level, and there was virtually no opportunity for staff to progress internally. These tend to be small organisations where no 'middle' positions (*ie* senior care workers) are available, thus making it difficult, if not impossible, for staff to gain the necessary experience to progress into management. In addition, regardless of size, most private agencies providing domiciliary care offer only basic grade positions.

For jobs at this level, research participants emphasised the importance of personal attributes and qualities. While care workers need to possess a range of core skills, most interviewees argued that these can be acquired during the induction period and with further on-the-job training. This distinction between personal attributes (which must be evident on recruitment) and skills (which can be learnt subsequently) is crucial for positions at this level, as one respondent explained:

> 'The work of care assistants requires a degree of skill, but personal qualities such as patience, understanding, respect and sense of humour are equally, if not more, important — this is not always fully appreciated.'

5.2.1 Personal skills and attributes

In describing the personal skills and attributes care workers are expected to have, one respondent said:

> 'Basically this is an occupation you have to have a feel for; people must want to do this type of job.'

Maturity, life experience and common sense are all regarded as essential in this type of work. However, maturity was conceived differently by different respondents; some believed that this requirement means that very young people (*ie* in their early/mid-20s or younger) are not suitable for the job. Others actively encouraged young people (including school leavers) to apply for these positions, as they believed that even young people can be sufficiently mature and have enough life experience to do the job.

An interest in people and an affinity with the elderly are also considered very important. However, some respondents warned about the common misconception that experience of working with children would automatically qualify one for work with the elderly. These are two different client groups with specific needs and requiring different approaches.

Care workers also need to be enthusiastic, motivated and have a sense of humour. These attributes are becoming particularly important, given the emphasis on avoiding routinisation and institutionalisation, and the need to provide a stimulating environment where elderly people can lead a fulfilling life.

Sensitivity, tactfulness, patience and the ability to remain calm are essential qualities given the variety of the sometimes painful and distressing situations that care workers have to deal with almost on a daily basis. For the same reason, adaptability, flexibility and initiative are also equally important, as one respondent put it:

> 'Care workers must be able to deal with whatever is thrown at them. When they walk into a client's home they can never fully anticipate what will be expected from them.'

Intuition is also considered important, as care workers must be able to assess and react to people and situations fairly quickly. At the same time, they must be able to take a holistic approach and assess a situation from different perspectives (for example the client as well as his/her relatives or main carer).

Reliability, honesty and the ability to keep information confidential are regarded as essential qualities. Many vulnerable people depend on the service provided by care workers, and reliability is therefore very important. Access to clients' homes, personal belongings and confidential information require people who are honest and discreet.

It is also important for care staff to understand boundaries, as one respondent explained:

> 'Care workers must know where to draw the line, what services and care they should and should not provide. For example, while they need to be sympathetic listeners and should provide emotional support, they should never try to provide counselling, as they are not trained to do this.'

Perhaps the most important quality of all emerging from the interviews is compassion: that is, the ability to treat others with respect, as one interviewee argued:

'The test we tell care workers to apply to everything they do, is to ask themselves whether they would be happy to be treated in that way, or if they would be happy if their mother or father were treated in that way. If they cannot answer positively, then the way they operate must be questioned and changed.'

5.2.2 Skill requirements

Care workers' tasks and related skills can be classified in four broad categories:

- personal care
- social care
- medical care
- domestic care.

The skills associated with these different types of care are discussed in turn below.

Personal care

Care staff have to carry out a number of personal care tasks, which might include helping clients to get up in the morning; assist with washing, bathing, dressing and undressing; and help with eating and drinking. The complexity of these tasks depends on the mental and physical abilities of the clients, with frail and confused people requiring heavier care and higher level skills. Care workers in day centres spend considerably less time on these tasks than their colleagues in domiciliary and residential care.

The skills required to carry out personal care tasks include:

- an awareness of correct procedures for carrying out personal care tasks, including techniques for lifting and handling, for transfers, bed moves, from floor, *etc.*
- dealing with incontinence
- using correct procedures for preparing, handling and maintaining equipment used in personal care.

The influence of recent health and safety legislation, and the need to protect both staff and clients, are clearly reflected in the emphasis employers now put on the need to follow correct procedures in carrying out personal care tasks.

Social care

In the old 'warehouse' model of care, the emphasis was mainly on personal care and ensuring that clients were 'washed, dressed and fed'. However, a more holistic approach to care places greater emphasis on social care and on responding to clients' emotional and psychological, as well as physical needs. This is perhaps the most complex area of work, where requirements have changed considerably in the past few years, and where care workers have to deal with some very difficult situations requiring a range of skills and knowledge. These include:

- an understanding of the function of the care plan and of key working, which in turn require the ability to gather, record and report information both orally and in writing
- an appreciation of the ageing process and its impact, and in particular the ability to understand how clients can make as full use as possible of their mental and physical capabilities
- an understanding of the needs of terminally ill clients and their family, and the bereavement process
- an ability to organise activities which provide clients with mental and physical stimulation
- an ability to communicate with a range of people, including clients, their relatives and other care professionals
- good listening and 'hearing' skills which imply a non-judgmental approach. As one respondent explained, a good care worker needs to be 'a sympathetic listener without attempting to be a counsellor'.
- an awareness of adult abuse, and more specifically the ability to identify possible signs of abuse, and report them to appropriate professionals or colleagues
- an awareness of equal opportunities, and an understanding of the practical implications of valuing and recognising diversity.

Some of these skills (eg communication and listening skills, ability to organise activities) have traditionally been more important in day centres, and to some extent in residential care. However, the research findings also show how care in the community is leading to a greater emphasis being placed on social care, even in domiciliary work. In particular, home care staff are increasingly seen as playing an important role in enabling clients to achieve maximum independence.

Medical care

The need to provide basic medical care is increasing in both residential homes and in domiciliary care. The emphasis on providing care for elderly people in the community has meant that those admitted to residential homes are older than they used to be, they are also very frail and likely to require heavy care. Respondents reported a substantial increase in the past few years in the level and complexity of medical care now required by clients in residential homes. Care staff, particularly in residential care and domiciliary services, are increasingly expected to provide basic medical care, and monitor and report to appropriate professionals any changes in clients' health. Specific skills and knowledge required in relation to medical care include:

- a basic knowledge of the use and abuse of drugs
- an understanding of the organisation's medication policy and the ability to follow correct procedures for the control, administration of drugs and the recording of their use
- an awareness of the range of the most common medical conditions affecting older people and an ability to provide basic assistance to clients with mental and physical problems, and disabilities. Examples of these include: speech therapy; communicating with people with hearing problems; dealing with mental health problems, such as memory loss, confusion and aggressive behaviour
- an ability to help clients to use and maintain care aids and other personal medical equipment
- basic first aid skills.

Domestic care

The ability to carry out a range of domestic chores has traditionally been the main requirement for home care staff. While in larger residential establishments these tasks might be carried out by domestic staff, residential care workers in smaller homes and occasionally in larger ones as well, are also expected to provide domestic care, including cleaning, cooking, serving meals, tidying up, *etc.* This aspect of the work has traditionally been seen as requiring good practical skills. However, the introduction of health and safety legislation has considerably changed the type of skills and knowledge linked to the provision of domestic care. In addition to carrying out a range of domestic tasks, care workers are now expected to provide a safe environment and to prevent risks. Specific skills and knowledge required include:

- an awareness of food hygiene and correct practices for handling food
- an understanding of practices for the safe use of, storage and handling of hazardous substances, and the use of personal protective equipment
- a knowledge of best practice in cases in infectious diseases and to prevent cross infection
- an awareness of prevention and risk assessment.

5.3 Senior care workers

At this level staff start moving away from the provision of direct care, and their job is more about ensuring that the care is provided according to organisational standards and procedures. Senior care workers are still involved in providing direct care, but the extent and nature of their involvement varies considerably across different settings and organisations. The research findings show that senior care workers do not normally have line management responsibilities, but they are likely to be responsible for organising and managing other people's work (for example organise rotas, supervise a team of care workers). In small residential homes, they might also occasionally be left in charge of a shift.

The findings show that relevant paid experience is normally required for senior care workers' positions. However, the length of experience can vary considerably. Many senior care staff are likely to be recruited internally.

Again, qualifications are likely to be desirable rather than essential requirements, with some evidence that NVQs at Levels 2 or 3 are becoming the qualifications more likely to be seen as relevant. While the historical development of the occupation means that even at this level qualifications are not usually required, some respondents emphasised that applicants for these positions are expected to have attended a wide range of relevant short courses and to have undertaken considerable on-the-job training.

Generally speaking, senior care posts seem more likely to be available in residential care, and in local authorities or large organisations in the independent sector. Most small or even medium sized voluntary and private organisations do not offer these 'intermediate positions', which are also being eliminated in domiciliary care in the statutory sector. For example, the sample included a local authority where senior home care assistant positions are being phased out, leaving a career structure with only two levels: domiciliary care assistant and domiciliary team leader, with a very wide gap between the two positions. It was anticipated that the removal of the 'middle' grade will reduce domiciliary care staff career opportunities. While in the past most domiciliary care managers came via the senior domiciliary worker route, in the future they are more likely to come from other sectors, as basic grade domiciliary staff will lack the necessary basic management experience required. Senior care worker positions seem also less likely to be available in day centres, but this is such a small area with so much variation in terms of the nature of work, range of tasks and responsibilities, that it was difficult to identify 'typical' occupational and career structures.

5.3.1 Skill requirements

As mentioned earlier, senior care workers normally progress to this position from a basic care post. Given their involvement with providing direct care, senior care workers are expected to have the personal attributes and core skills required at basic level. A crucial difference between the two levels is that while basic level staff are not required to possess all or even most of the core skills on recruitment, senior staff are expected to have acquired and developed these skills to a high level in a previous care post(s).

Most senior care workers play a crucial role in the implement-ation of clients' care plan. They therefore require an ability to collect the necessary information to monitor the care plan, ensure it is fully implemented and take action in case of problems.

Senior care workers must have good oral and written communi-cation skills as reporting information (particularly related to the care plan) to other professionals, colleagues, clients and their relatives is increasingly an important aspect of their job.

Staff at this level must also be good organisers and have some basic administration skills. Team working is very important in all care settings and it is essential for senior staff to be able to co-ordinate the work of different team members. With the greater emphasis being placed on following correct procedures (for example in relation to health and safety or medication policies) and recording and storing all the necessary information, administration skills are also becoming important.

Senior care workers must be able to delegate, and in particular they must be able to judge when other staff have the necessary skills and knowledge to carry out certain tasks, and when it would not be appropriate to ask them to do so.

Staff at this level are also expected to develop people management skills as they supervise care staff work, and may even lead a small team of people.

5.4 Managers

This level includes deputy or assistant managers, as well as head of homes, day centres and home care organisers. These are, to all intents and purposes, management jobs. The research findings show that in the voluntary and statutory organisations, only people with some management experience in the care sector are regarded as suitable for these positions. However, in some private organisations, 'outsiders' from the business sector are regarded equally, if not more suitable for the job. This was particularly true for private domiciliary care agencies.

The complexity of the nature of the work and tasks at the management level can vary considerably: from the head of a small day centre managing a very small budget and a small group of staff, to the head of a residential home managing a budget of £1.5 million and a large group of staff. Deputy level posts can also vary considerably in terms of level of respon- sibility. For example, in one local authority, assistant managers were playing a vital role in the day-to-day management of residential homes, as typically there would be one manager responsible for three homes, therefore relying heavily on the support of assistant managers.

Relevant management experience is always required for these posts. However, as discussed earlier, only in public and voluntary organisations has this to be specifically related to the care sector. Nurses are often found in management positions in residential care. This is a legal requirement for nursing homes. However, at a time when residents are more likely to require medical care, qualified nurses are increasingly seen as suitable, even in residential homes.

Qualifications are far more likely to be required for management positions, but the sample included organisations which did not regard them as essential even at this level. The most common professional qualifications expected for these positions included social work, nursing, or more general qualifications in social welfare. The shift towards the mixed economy of care, increased competition, and the drive towards greater efficiency have meant that general management qualifications are also becoming more important in all sectors and settings.

As mentioned earlier, in local authorities, longer career structures and better training and development opportunities (including the availability of secondment to qualifying courses) have meant that a small number of care staff have traditionally had the opportunity to climb the career ladder and move into management posts. However, opportunities vary between different settings, and generally speaking, residential work has provided better career opportunities than domiciliary care or day centres. The picture in the independent sector is more mixed, and here career opportunities depend very much on the size of the employer. In small organisations lacking 'middle' level positions it is very difficult, if not impossible, for care workers to progress into management. Large voluntary organisations and some private sector employers offer development and career opportunities similar to those available in local authorities, supported by similar training opportunities. However, some private sector employers offer little or no opportunities for development to their care staff, and very little training. This seems to be particularly the case in domiciliary care agencies.

5.4.1 Skill requirements for managers

Requirements at this level reflect the type of skills normally required in management posts. These include:

- a knowledge of a range of personnel issues
- good people management skills: these are essential as the job involves supporting staff who often work under stressful and difficult conditions

- leadership skills: these are particularly important given that residential homes and day centres tend to operate relatively autonomously, as one respondent explained:

  'Good homes, where you find the best examples of good practice, are always run by a very good manager who leads from the front and provides a sense of direction.'

- financial skills: these are becoming increasingly important because of the need to operate in an increasingly competitive market, and to reduce costs and maximise efficiency.

As mentioned earlier, views vary regarding managers' need to have good care skills and previous 'hands on' experience of providing care. However, the majority of respondents regarded these as essential, and would expect managers to have developed the core skills expected from more junior staff to a very high level.

5.5 Changing skill needs

The research findings clearly illustrate how skill requirements and competency levels are changing rapidly in response to the recent legislative and cultural developments discussed in Chapter 3. An increasingly frail and older population requires more complex and heavier care than in the past. In particular, personal care tasks are becoming more complex and the amount and level of medical care required have also increased. Growing concern about workers' and clients' safety, and legal requirements, have also led to changes in the skills and knowledge workers must have. Many care tasks now have to be carried out in compliance with health and safety legislation.

While a frailer client group and health and safety requirements have influenced mainly competency levels, the shift to an holistic and client focused approach to care provision has had a considerable impact on the nature and range of skill requirements. The greater emphasis on broader requirements is particularly apparent in residential homes, where traditionally the emphasis had been on meeting clients' physical needs, and in domiciliary care where staff were often seen as 'glorified servants'. In residential homes, the need to create a stimulating environment and to spend 'quality' time with clients (for example to listen, provide emotional support, *etc.*) is seen as increasingly important, and not as simply marginal and *ad hoc* activities to be carried out if and when there is time. These new needs and demands require a wider range of social, creative and interpersonal skills which were not normally seen as necessary when the focus was on personal care and meeting residents' physical needs. There has also been a considerable shift in the nature of domiciliary work, with frailer people requiring substantial care now more likely to be cared for at home. Staff in this setting are increasingly asked to provide personal and medical care, as well as emotional and psychological support. Again, this type of care requires a wider range of skills and abilities than were traditionally expected, when the job was mainly confined to domestic chores.

The need for care providers to survive in an increasingly competitive market is also leading to changes in expectations about the type and level of skill requirements. In line with more general organisational changes, care providers (particularly in the statutory sector) are trying to reduce costs and improve efficiency by creating flatter organisational structures. In some cases, this has led to the elimination of senior care worker positions. This means that many staff at basic level have more and broader responsibilities, and require higher competency levels.

In order to remain competitive, care providers also need to be increasingly flexible and creative, and again flexibility and creativity require staff with a broader range of skills. For example, the study included a local authority which is planning to combine different types of services in order to provide a 'continuum of care'. That is, a key worker will provide care to clients in different settings according to their requirements. This system will require care staff to have the necessary skills and knowledge to operate in residential and domiciliary settings, as well as day centres.

In an attempt to find a niche in an increasingly competitive market, some local authorities are also considering the possibilities of focusing on the provision of 'specialist' care (for example respite care, rehabilitation and specialised units), where there is little competition from the independent sector. The provision of specialist care requires staff with considerably higher skill levels in specific areas (such as rehabilitation and mental health).

Finally, increasing flexibility and diversification could also mean that many care staff will have to work with different client groups. In a local authority included in the study, care staff who had traditionally provided elder care, were beginning to provide a service to families at risk and people with a disability. While some core skills are common to the provision of care to different client groups, some requirements are specific to particular groups, and again will require care staff to broaden their skill portfolio.

These changes in skill requirements have considerable implications for training and recruitment strategies, particularly since this is still, by and large, an unqualified and poorly trained workforce. In addition, poor pay and working conditions mean that it is unlikely that the occupation will succeed in attracting better educated and qualified staff. The findings on recruitment and skill gaps are discussed in the second part of Chapter 6, while Chapter 7 highlights some of the main issues in relation to training opportunities for care staff.

6. Recruitment and Shortages

6.1 Introduction

This chapter briefly explores issues around the recruitment of caring staff and the difficulties in obtaining staff. The first section looks at childcare and the second at caring for elderly people. There are a number of similarities between the two sectors of caring. We came across examples of well thought out and defined recruitment procedures, and heard of many other examples where procedures were at best *ad hoc*.

6.2 Recruitment in the childcare sector

6.2.1 Recruitment

Our findings suggest that recruitment procedures and practices vary greatly, as does the extent to which childcare providers are adopting more professional approaches. Many of the managers we spoke to were able to report fairly well structured recruitment procedures, and we were given a number of examples of clear job descriptions and specifications.

The nature of the recruitment process and selection criteria did depend on the type of job being filled and the balance of staff already existing. Nurseries are required to have at least half their staff with a childcare qualification. If a manager was looking to replace a member of their qualified staff who had left or to increase the balance of qualified staff, an applicant would need to have a relevant qualification as a minimum. NNEB and BTEC were most commonly mentioned, but as NVQs become more widespread they are also considered. Apart from this, qualifications were not seen as very important, although increasingly managers reported that they are looking for staff who are prepared to work towards a childcare qualification.

In this study, unlike in some others, we did not explore in great depth the criteria managers used when recruiting staff. However, the recruitment interview was very important. At this interview, managers tried to explore why the applicant wanted to work with children and their approach to childcare, assessing whether or not they had the appropriate attitudes and approach to fit into that particular nursery or playgroup. Recruiting people who would 'fit in' was particularly emphasised. This also meant fitting in with existing staff and being able to work effectively in a team with them.

Greater awareness of the skills and knowledge desirable in childcare workers is leading to more thought being given to the recruitment process. However, this also requires managers to develop a new set of skills, in interviewing and assessment. It is difficult to draw any firm conclusions from our data about the extent to which this is happening. However, it seems there is still a long way to go. When a company is running a number of different nurseries, there is possibly greater potential for procedures to be established and managers trained in these. However, many managers are running their own small business. This creates particular problems in establishing a set of skills and procedures. Not only is more detailed interviewing and assessment a skill these managers are not always aware of the need for, but our (limited) evidence suggests that many people running nurseries do not see any need to change their practices.

A further difficulty in establishing a set of recruitment procedures is that many people working with children are directly recruited and employed by parents. Some parents might have been involved in recruiting staff in their job, but for many others, recruiting someone to look after their children might be their first experience. Many idiosyncrasies, for example, are likely to emerge and in the end, the decision might rest on whether or not the parents and carer 'hit it off'. Some parents will have definite views about how their children should be brought up, which might conflict with what is generally considered to be good practice. Others might have no particular view as long as their children are happy, safe and well.

Childminders have to register with their local authority. This often involves only a police check. Many authorities do not look for evidence of knowledge and skills in childminding. This is, however, beginning to change. The Children Act and more general concerns about the quality of care provided for young children are contributing to changes in practices. The National Childminding Association has developed a leaflet and a video which tries to help parents identify what they should be looking for when choosing a childminder. However, there is still a long way to go before there are high levels of expectation in skills and recruitment. It was commented during the course of our interviews that although children are regarded as a precious thing, this does not always seem to be followed through in their care.

Generally, retention of staff was not reported to be an issue among our sample. However, it is likely that our interviews were with providers who would be regarded as high quality, and who were more likely to have thought through their needs and recruitment. Indeed, one respondent did report that they paid well, had a good reputation and a team that worked together well — neither recruitment nor retention were presenting them with problems.

6.2.2 Skill gaps and shortages

As increasing emphasis is placed on the skills needed of childcarers and the need for a professional approach, gaps and shortages seem likely to emerge. Some respondents did report that they found applicants with experience in some types of provision lacked certain areas of expertise and knowledge. It was generally reported that as many nurseries, for example, are run by women who trained in childcare some time ago, there is an inertia towards change. Not all people keep up to date with changes in approach to looking after children, or see the changes being made as important, especially if parents are not demanding them. The introduction of Nursery Education Vouchers contributed to a change in this, as providers became aware of the need to more consciously think about the service they offered to be eligible to take vouchers. Another push for change might be the development of a more skilled workforce entering the occupation, as the initial training changes.

We did not come across major reports of skill shortages or difficulties in recruiting, but there were a number of particular areas of knowledge or skill in which there were felt to be general weaknesses. These included:

- the understanding and application of equal opportunity policies
- true understanding of child development and the role of play in learning

- relating to parents and families
- basic skills — as the educational and developmental role of childcare receives emphasis, the basic skills of childcarers become more important. Several respondents reported that job applicants frequently had poor levels of literacy and numeracy.

6.3 Recruitment and caring for elderly people

6.3.1 Recruitment and retention

The research findings show that recruitment procedures and practices vary enormously. At one end of the spectrum some local authorities are developing competency frameworks for care staff, and have fairly detailed job descriptions clearly specifying basic skill requirements. Larger organisations in the independent sector also tend to have established procedures for advertising positions both externally and internally, and for the shortlisting, interviewing and appointing of care staff. In some cases, clients are also involved in the recruitment process. This was most likely to be informal (for example, showing the applicants around the home, and having a chat with them). However, in some organisations, clients' feedback on applicants is gathered, and examples of clients being included in interviewing panels were also reported.

At the other extreme, there were some 'horror' stories of job applicants being interviewed and appointed over the telephone, and given a list of clients to visit straight away. These are extreme and possibly rare cases. However, informal recruitment methods have traditionally been widespread in the care sector in general, and frequently little emphasis has been put on skill requirements or job descriptions. As one respondent explained, in relation to the type of the requirements expected by some small private sector employers:

> 'Requirements in some cases are very basic and all that an employer wants is someone who can iron, clean, cook and who doesn't steal.'

These research findings show contrasting pressures on the ways in which staff are recruited. On the one hand, equal opportunities policies, the development of occupational standards, the increased emphasis on competencies and qualifications, are all having a positive influence on the recruitment process. On the other hand, the pressure to cut costs and the growing number of very small care providers may mean that informal recruitment practices will remain widespread. Recruitment methods and practices have a considerable influence on the quality of staff recruited, which in turn determines the quality of the service provided. Some respondents expressed concern about the widespread use of informal recruitment practices, particularly among some private domiciliary care agencies. Unlike residential care, this service is totally unregulated and minimum standards (for example, in relation to health and safety and the type of care provided) are not legally set out.

Recruitment and retention difficulties were only explored briefly in this study. Local authorities tend to offer higher pay levels than private and voluntary employers. Working conditions, development, and training opportunities are also generally regarded as good in local authorities. However, they can vary considerably in the independent sector. In this sector, the quality and amount of training and career opportunities depend very much on the size of the organisation, with the majority of smaller employers offering very little in that respect.

Given that local authorities are able to offer better pay and working conditions, they are the least likely to experience recruitment and retention difficulties. However, some local authorities are experiencing high turnover and retention problems in domiciliary services. These problems are believed to be partly linked to the nature of the job in this setting, where people work in isolation, with little contact or support from their manager and colleagues. In addition, the emphasis on providing a service when clients need it, rather than when it is convenient for the provider, means that increasingly home care staff have to work at weekends and unsocial hours. The job has also become more demanding and stressful because of the greater emphasis on social and medical care. Furthermore, on the whole, local authorities are not able to offer adequate financial rewards and promotion opportunities to reflect the greater demands of the job.

Recruitment and retention seem more likely to represent a problem for providers in the independent sector. However, the picture is rather mixed. Private domiciliary care agencies reported the same difficulties experienced by local authorities, with turnover rates being even higher in this sector. In the residential homes, problems tend to arise in specific geographical locations. That is, traditional retirement areas where there is a high demand for care staff. Some voluntary organisations find it increasingly hard to compete with private employers who might offer a slightly higher level of pay (and differentiated pay levels according to geographical areas), but provide little or no training and development opportunities. In a sector where pay levels are so low, many people will opt for higher rates of pay, even if this is at the expense of training opportunities. This represents a problem for voluntary organisations who place a greater emphasis on training and development in line with their organisational policies and strategies.

6.3.2 Skill gaps

The main skill gaps emerging from the study are related to the cultural and legislative changes mentioned earlier, and the demand for more complex care.

Despite the emphasis care providers now put on values such as dignity, empowerment and privacy, some staff attitudes are hard to change. The research findings show that there is still a tendency among some care staff to patronise clients; fail to respect their privacy (*eg* walk into bedrooms without knocking, or discuss clients' private affairs with others); assume that staff know what is best for clients; and have rigid ideas about what clients can and cannot do. Some respondents believed that the lack of a full appreciation of these values and the failure to put them into practice are more evident in relation to clients suffering from dementia. In many cases there seems to be a lack of understanding as to the nature of this illness and how to deal with people who suffer from dementia.

An awareness of equal opportunities policies and practices was also described by one respondent as 'a massive gap'. While it was recognised that there has been an improvement in this area in recent years, with many organisations offering relevant training and advice, it is believed that many care staff still lack a theoretical and practical understanding of key equal opportunities issues.

Some respondents also expressed concern about the lack of understanding of some key policies and procedures introduced to maximise the quality of the care provided and to be more responsive to clients' needs. These include the care plan and key working. It was felt that while staff might have been given some training on these issues, this has tended to be superficial, and many care workers lack a true understanding of the purpose of the care plan and the keyworking system. In particular, it was felt that many staff do not really appreciate the role a client's history should play in informing the care that they receive.

As discussed earlier, basic medical care is increasingly required in both residential homes and domiciliary services, and some of the skill gaps emerging from the study relate to these new demands. For example, the use of medication was identified by some interviewees as an area where more needs to be done, to ensure that all staff understand correct procedures for administering drugs, and the importance of record keeping. Some respondents also argued that there is a problem around the abuse and misuse of drugs, particularly in relation to clients with mental health problems.

As the elderly population is getting older and frailer, rehabilitation is becoming increasingly important, but it was believed that in many cases the tendency is still to under-estimate what clients can do, and care workers tend to be 'over-protective'. There is also a gap around basic rehabilitation skills (for example, speech therapy, and physiotherapy) and the use of personal equipment, such as hearing and walking aids.

Finally, as the need to gather and record information for various purposes (for example, health and safety, care plan) is increasing, literacy skills are becoming more important. Traditionally, care workers have not been expected to be able to communicate in writing, and this was identified as a big gap. One respondent explained:

> 'Care staff are fearful of writing reports. Many have not written anything since they left school and they have no confidence at all in their writing abilities.'

However, this problem does not seem to be confined to older care workers, and it was reported that many younger staff also had difficulties meeting the basic literacy skills now required in the occupation.

7. Training and Development

7.1 Introduction

A theme throughout this report has been the low value placed on the skills needed in these two areas of caring, which both in their own way are increasingly requiring a higher level of skill and knowledge of workers. The evidence suggests that the majority of people working in childcare, and particularly, caring for the elderly, are unqualified. It has long been assumed that caring is an innate, usually female activity, which comes to people naturally. Training has therefore not been seen as very important. However, our evidence does suggest that this is beginning to change. A number of our respondents reported that greater attention was being paid to training and development, and the availability of training opportunities had improved in recent years.

7.2 Childcare

Within the childcare sector, there is some degree of regulation, but this is inconsistent. For example, although at least half the staff in nurseries have to be qualified, people registering as childminders do not have to show evidence of receiving any formal training. One respondent pointed out that to work with food, one needs a food hygiene certificate, but to work with children there are very few requirements. A recent survey (Moss et al., 1995) of 419 day care providers in England and Wales, found that the most frequent qualification among heads of nurseries and nursery staff was the NNEB. Playgroup workers most frequently attended courses run by the Pre-school Learning Alliance and other agencies. One-third of playgroup workers and one-fifth of day nursery staff had no relevant qualifications. Moss et al. (1995) also concluded:

'The great majority of childminders had no relevant qualifications.'

Our research found that although many childcare workers did not have any qualification in childcare, there was a greater awareness of the need for training, and that staff in nurseries, for example, were attending a range of different courses. In a few cases, considerable emphasis was being placed on staff becoming qualified, and the NVQ, with its competence based structure and methods of assessment, was opening up opportunities for this.

Much training is provided through short courses and is on very practical issues, for example, first aid, food handling, health and safety. There are also courses which aim to develop personal competencies. A few of our respondents ran nurseries, or some other types of provision which were part of a larger organisation. They often reported that this offered more scope for providing training. There was an infrastructure which could offer administration in setting up courses and there were a larger number of staff able to attend courses. More resources were generally available than to managers of single nurseries.

It was those working alone who experienced fewest opportunities for training. Childminders and nannies, for example, might rarely find opportunities to develop or update their skills. Some local authorities do run various types of training course and the National Childminding Association is looking at ways in which this issue can be addressed.

Many of the people we spoke to during the course of this research reported that there was a need for more training. Attempts were being made to raise awareness of the importance of training and enable more people to participate. For example, CACHE (Council for Awards in Childcare and Education) offers distance learning for all their awards. They are also looking at ways of providing a range of levels of training, involving different time commitments, to cater for different needs.

A number of problems and barriers were identified. In particular, the cost of training and the time involved were mentioned. Many types of childcare provision do not draw in levels of income that allow much flexibility in paying for courses and providing cover while staff attend courses. Furthermore, although some managers might value staff putting their own money and time into training, this is not always the case. We heard of an example where no recognition was given to a member of staff who had paid to attend training courses herself. Childcare is a low paid occupation, and there is little career progression and few opportunities for higher pay which might recompense someone paying for their own training. Many childcare workers also have their own family responsibilities and limited time to devote to training outside work.

An additional and important barrier identified by many professionals was the attitude to training of many people, especially managers, working in childcare. An attitude prevails that:

> 'We are trained and we know it all anyway.'

It was reported that there is a resistance to seeing training as an on-going process. Many managers, including those running their own nursery, apparently do not appreciate the extent to which there is a changing body of knowledge and expertise around the care and development of children. This possibly relates to a more general attitude that looking after children is something which is basically innate. Other studies in this series have illustrated the importance of managers in driving change. Where this is not forthcoming, practices are slow to change. An additional factor is the role of parents as employers in the childcare sector. It was reported that many parents do not realise or appreciate changes occurring in the skills and knowledge relevant to childcare. The training and development provided to carers is not something they will necessarily look at in selecting a nursery or childminder, for example. Indeed, one respondent reported coming across a business which was mostly staffed by unskilled and unsupervised staff, and trainees:

> 'Babies were being looked after by children, not skilled workers. Parents are wonderfully naive.'

7.3 Elder care

As discussed earlier, training opportunities in the occupation tend to be limited and vary considerably according to setting, sector and employer size.

The research findings show that local authorities and many large providers in the independent sector offer a range of training opportunities, which normally include an induction programme, external and internal courses as well as on-the-job training. In local authorities, the opportunity to be seconded to qualifying courses (eg Certificate of Qualification in Social Work, Certificate in Social Services, Diploma in Social Work) has also traditionally been available to a small proportion of care workers. However, before the introduction of NVQs, the overwhelming majority of training available was in the form of short courses and on-the-job training.

Given the tendency to recruit people with the 'right attitude' but who might lack many of the core skills and knowledge required in the occupation, induction programmes play a very important role. The study included organisations who offered comprehensive induction programmes, normally lasting between four and eight days. These tend to cover three broad areas:

The organisation's approach to care delivery

- organisational values
- key working and care planning
- admission and discharge (for residential staff only).

Policies and procedures

- equal opportunities
- health and safety
- medication
- carrying out personal care tasks
- adult abuse
- record keeping.

Working with the elderly

- managing difficult and aggressive behaviour
- common medical conditions affecting elderly people
- dealing with terminally ill people, loss and bereavement.

More specialist courses and staff seminars are also offered by these organisations on more specific and specialist issues, such as:

- rehabilitation
- dementia care

- stress management
- organising activities and occupational therapy
- working with elderly people with disabilities.

The introduction of NVQs has contributed to organisations developing more systematic ways of identifying skill needs and gaps. These will be used to develop appropriate training programmes. Most of the larger organisations included in the study are setting up NVQ programmes, with basic level staff encouraged to take Level 2, and senior care workers Level 3. However, limited resources and the large number of unqualified staff mean that it will take many years before most care workers will obtain an NVQ or another equivalent qualification. A recent survey of care staff in social services departments conducted by the National Institute for Social Work (NISW) presents an even less optimistic picture. The survey findings show that 40 per cent of care staff had not heard of NVQs. Of those who had, only 43 per cent said they could definitely be assessed through their department. Only 11 per cent of those who could be assessed through their department either held or were taking an NVQ. The researchers concluded that:

'These findings suggest that NVQs are not widely known about in social services departments, and that the opportunities for unqualified staff to obtain these qualifications remain limited.'
(Balloch *et al.*, 1995)

Our research findings and the NISW survey show that qualified training is still only available to a minority of care workers in local authorities. However, by and large, social services departments and most large providers in the independent sector do offer some basic training and induction programmes, which help staff to develop the essential knowledge and core skills required in the occupation. Our findings also show that a lack of adequate training remains a big problem among providers in the independent sector, particularly among the medium and small ones. Some extreme examples were reported of private organisations providing no induction or subsequent training. This seems particularly to be a problem in domiciliary care, as mentioned earlier. This sector is not regulated and there is therefore no incentive to provide even basic training and information on policies and procedure on health and safety, personal and health care.

Lack of resources was mentioned as a problem in relation to inadequate training. Competition is intensifying and providers have to cut costs to remain competitive. It is therefore increasingly difficult to fund training. While this seems to be a problem for all providers, it affects small organisations in particular, as they do not have access to central training budgets and lack the knowledge and time to tap into external sources of funding. Some respondents (particularly in the independent sector) also believed that Training and Enterprise Councils (TECs) have failed to assist a sector where there is such an obvious need for training. According to these interviewees, this 'neglect' is mainly due to the fact that the TECs' work is mainly focused on the under 25s, and since the overwhelming majority of care staff working with the elderly are older, they do not qualify for assistance under most of the TECs' programmes.

8. Discussion

This study looked at two areas of caring: childcare, in particular pre-school childcare, and eldercare. A number of themes emerge from the two strands of our investigation. Caring occupations have traditionally been seen as requiring little skill and training. Our study shows that each involves a specific body of skill and knowledge. The overall conclusion is that there are more differences than similarities in the nature of skills needed in each. However, there are many similarities in terms of the characteristics and status of those working in the two sectors.

A common theme relating to both these occupations is the traditional lack of recognition and undervaluing of the skills involved. Caring for young children and elderly people has long been perceived to involve little real skill and need little training. Caring, as argued in Chapter 2, is often considered innate, something which comes naturally to particular groups of people, especially women. The continued predominance of women in the workforce has also contributed to an under-mining of the skills involved. Historically, it is occupations involving a degree of technical skill and a training period during which these skills are acquired, which are considered skilled. These occupations were usually male dominated. The caring activities explored here and to some extent others which do require a period of training, have not been seen as falling into the same category as more technical work. This is perpetuated in recent occupational classifications.

In addition, those entering caring occupations have often contributed to this lack of recognition of the skills involved. For example, Penn and McQuail (1997) found that many female students in their study had chosen childcare training because they saw it as easy and unthreatening, building on skills they thought they already possessed.

Our evidence does show how these caring occupations do require a particular body of skill and knowledge. Some of these are common to both, however there are also many differences. A range of personal qualities and abilities are very important in both areas of caring, although their application may be different. Carers also need the skills and abilities which enable them to operate in a work context and with colleagues. In addition, each occupation has its own specific requirements, illustrated in detail in Chapters 4 and 5. Carers contribute to the personal, educational and emotional development of the children they are responsible for, through providing opportunities to learn, managing behaviours and so on. Working with elderly people involves providing social care, through responding to a client's emotional and psychological needs, and medical care.

At the time of our fieldwork there was pressure from many professionals to create a separate National Training Organisation (NTO) for childcare. Others were reported to believe that the skill requirements were similar across all, or most, caring occupations and that no NTO could cater for them all. What this study clearly shows is the extent of difference in skill needs. Indeed, some respondents in the eldercare part of this study warned about a common misconception that experience of working with children would automatically qualify someone to work with elderly people. The two different client groups have specific needs requiring varying approaches.

The list of personal attributes and skills needed was very similar for both caring occupations, and indeed a similar list is likely to emerge for many occupations. However, the context in which these attributes and skills are used does vary between occupations and organisations. Although the principles behind team working, for example, are likely to be similar in most organisations, other personal skills need to be applied in a way relevant to meeting the needs of a particular client group. For example, communication skills need to be appropriate to the people being spoken to. Young children and elderly people should all be treated individually and as people. However, the precise nature of communication with each will be different.

There is a small degree of overlap in the specific skills needed to work with young children and elderly people. For example, administration skills and the ability to record information are increasingly important: first aid, basic hygiene, and health and safety are all relevant. However the main skill and knowledge requirements are very different. The ability to help children develop and to manage child behaviour, for example, is very different from having the ability to provide a stimulating environment for an elderly, possibly infirm, person.

In addition to carers requiring specific skills and knowledge, the skills and knowledge needed are growing and changing. A more complex world, legislation and government policy, general attitudes and expectations in society have contributed to new and greater demands being placed on carers.

Apart from a move away from a traditional emphasis on physical caring, this aspect of caring has become more complex. There is considerable publicity when anything happens to young children, and there is considerable onus on childcarers in identifying and preventing damage occurring. In providing physical care for elderly people, more equipment is used and personal care tasks are more complex.

The greater emphasis on encouraging the psychological, emotional and educational development of pre-school children, and in caring for the social and emotional needs of elderly people, means that carers need the skills and knowledge to do this. However, these skills and knowledge are not static. New theoretical perspectives and ways of putting these into practice evolve over time, as more is understood about human behaviour, and expectations and attitudes in society change. Carers need to keep up with developments in their own particular field.

Basic skills, particularly literacy but also numeracy, are increasingly important in both caring occupations. Legislative changes have resulted in the need for more record keeping, in relation to care plans for the elderly and the progress of pre-school children. In addition, the educational aspect of pre-school care is receiving emphasis, and carers need basic skills themselves if they are to help young children develop these. Respondents expressed particular concern about a lack of confidence with numbers among childcarers.

Training and development

Both childcare and eldercare are dominated by a relatively unqualified workforce. It is not just a lack of vocational qualifications. Carers also tend to have obtained few academic qualifications while at school. Although there have long been qualifications available for people wanting to work with young children, these have by no means been a requirement for entry into the occupation. Indeed, many enter with little, if any, instruction or experience of dealing with children.

Better recognition of the skills needed in caring for pre-school children and elderly people is providing pressure for more training. This is being supported by developments in national policy, in particular the introduction of NTOs and sectoral qualification targets. The involvement of the Training and Enterprise Councils (TECs) in grant funding out-of-school clubs is having a major impact on this sector of childcare, and a knock-on effect on pre-school childcare. However, there is still a very long way to go before the training and development of those working with pre-school children and, in particular, elderly people becomes a matter of course. Pressures on costs and the development of a private sector market in eldercare do not help. The tradition of low training levels also tends to be self-perpetuating. For example, respondents in the childcare part of our study reported some resistance to the need for training among people who had either trained some time ago, or who had done well without receiving any training. They could not see a particular need for training and development, particularly any on-going training and development.

In the overall provision of care, it will only be when parents and relatives see evidence of qualifications and training as essential that the situation is likely to change to a large extent. A trained and qualified workforce does, however, have cost implications: an issue which is returned to below.

Pressures for and barriers to change

Chapters 2 and 3 reported a range of pressures for change in both childcare and eldercare. The root of these pressures was similar. They are based around changes in demographic and family structures, the increased participation of women in paid employment, and more general political and social attitudes. The pressure for change is unlikely to diminish, but the focus may change over time, as new developments, attitudes and political imperatives emerge. These pressures are all creating a greater demand for both pre-school childcare and eldercare. They are also broadening and deepening the skills required.

Many respondents talked about a need to recognise the skills required in caring occupations. They talked about a 'professional-isation' of care, the need to change attitudes and to recognise that caring is a skilled job: one which requires training and development.

However, despite pressures for change and the growing recognition of the skills required in caring jobs, there are a number of barriers to upgrading their status and position. Both caring occupations are dominated by relatively unqualified, almost exclusively female workforces, who receive some of the lowest wages in the economy. Cost pressures were reported by respondents from a range of different types of provision in both areas of care. Some of these pressures are a consequence of efforts to reduce public expenditure, or at least keep it under control. However, others are due to the extent to which people are prepared to pay for these services. Indeed, several managers and professionals we spoke to in the childcare sector commented on the relatively low level of fees parents were prepared to pay. This was very evident in a recent study of out-of-school childcare provision in Kent (Dench and O'Regan, 1998). A club manager reported that parents were not interested so much in whether the staff were qualified, experienced or police checked, but asked 'how much do you charge?' In some circumstances, this is related to their ability to pay. However, it seems to be the equation of childcare with domestic labour, and a lack of preparedness to recognise that skills are involved and to pay for these, which is a major cause. In recent years, media attention has highlighted a number of concerns about the quality of care provided for young children, and indeed elderly people. Yet untrained and inexperienced carers continue to be employed and given major responsibilities.

It seems that a major change in society's attitudes and values is needed if caring is to be upgraded, in terms of pay and status in particular, but also training provision. One of the major arguments used to persuade individuals of the advantages of training and development, and the necessity for them to take some personal responsibility in this area, is that training leads to greater rewards. These rewards are not all financial, but also include more interesting work, promotion and status. Other studies, for example on out-of-school childcare, illustrate that people working in childcare are prepared to train. However, few can afford to pay for themselves, especially when it is unlikely to lead to greater returns, in terms of pay or promotion.

The Institute for Employment Studies

Bibliography

Balloch S, Andrew T, Ginn J, McLean J, Pahl J, Williams J (1995), *Working in the Social Services*, National Institute for Social Work (NISW)

Barnes M, Wistow G (1992), 'Sustaining Innovation in Community Care', *Local Government Policy Making*, Vol. 18, No. 4

Challis D, Hugman R (1993), 'Community Care, Social Work and Social Care', *British Journal of Social Work*, Vol. 23, No. 4

Cohen B (1988), *Caring for Children — Services and Policies for Childcare and Equal Opportunities in the UK*, Report for the European Commission's Childcare Network

Cohen B (1990), *Caring for Children — The 1990s Report*, Report for the European Commission's Childcare Network on Childcare Services and Policy in the UK, Family Policy Studies Centre

Corti L, Laurie H, Dex S (1994), *Caring and Employment*, ESRC Research Centre on micro-social change, Employment Department Research Series No. 39

Corti L, Dex S (1995), 'Informal carers and employment', *Employment Gazette*, March, pp. 101-107

Dench S, O'Regan S (1998), *Helping Parents to Work: a study for Kent TEC*, IES Report 348

Department for Education and Employment (1996), *Work and Family: Ideas and Options for Childcare*. A consultative paper, DfEE, London

Department of Education and Science (1990), *Starting with Quality*, The Report of the Committee of Inquiry into the quality of the Educational experience offered to 3 and 4 year olds, London, HMSO

DHSSI (Department of Health Social Services Inspectorate) (1991), *Women in Social Services: A Neglected Resource*, HMSO

Elfer P, Beasley G (1997), A Law Unto Themselves? A survey of appeals and prosecutions under Part X of the Children Act 1989, concerning childminding and day care provision. National Children's Bureau, London

Finlayson L, Ford R, Marsh A (1996), 'Paying more for child care', *Labour Market Trends*, July, pp. 295-303

Giles L, La Valle I, Evans C (1996), *An Evaluation of the CENTEC Childcare Project*, unpublished IES Report

Holland D (1995), 'Pay, conditions and status — do they matter?', *Childcare Now*, The magazine of the Daycare Trust and the National Childcare Campaign, 15, 4

Holtermann S, Clarke T (1992), *Parents' employment rights and childcare — The Costs and Benefits of improved provision*, Equal Opportunities Commission

IRS (1996), 'Workplace childcare: the state of playing', *IRS Employment Trends* No. 622, December

Langman M (1990), 'Community Care in the 1990s: The Community Care White Paper: "Caring for People"', *Critical Social Policy*, Vol. 10, No. 2

La Valle I, Lyons K (1996), 'The Social Worker Speaks, I: Perception of Recent Changes in British Social Work', *Practice*, Vol. 8, No. 8

Local Government Management Board/Association of Directors of Social Services (1993), *Social Services Workforce Analysis 1992*

Marsh A, McKay S (1993), 'Families, work and the use of childcare', *Employment Gazette*, 101(8) pp. 361-370

Martin J, Roberts C (1984), *Women and Employment*, HMSO

McRae S (1991), *Maternity Rights in Britain: the PSI Report on the Experiences of Women and Employers*, Policy Studies Institute, London

McGlone F, Cronin N (1994), *A Crisis in Care — The Future of family and state care for older people in the European Union*, Family Policy Studies Centre/Centre for Policy on Ageing

Meijovogel R, Petrie P (eds) (1996), *School age childcare in the European Union*, European Commission Network on Childcare

Moss P (co-ordinator) (1990), *Childcare in the European Communities 1985-1990*, Women of Europe Supplements, No. 31, August

Moss P, Melhuish E (eds) (1991), *Current Issues in Day Care for Young Children*, HMSO

Moss P (1991), Day Care for Young Children in the UK in Melhuish E, Moss P (eds) Day for Young Children, International Perspective, Routledge, London

Moss P, *et al.* (1995), *Survey of Day Care Providers in England and Wales*, Thomas Coram Research Unit, London

Moss P (1996), in Meijovogel R, Petrie P (eds), *School age childcare in the European Union*, European Commission Network on Childcare

O'Brien M, Dench S (1996), *The Out-of School Childcare Grant Initiative*, Department for Education and Employment Research Report 72

ONS (1996), *New Earnings Survey*, HMSO, London

Penn H, McQuail S (1997), *Childcare as a Gendered Occupation*, Department for Education and Employment Research Report 23

Pugh G (ed) (1992), *Contemporary Issues in the Early Years*, Paul Chapman Publishing

Pugh G (ed.) (1996), *Education and Training for Work in the Early Years*, National Children's Bureau, London

Rai D K (1994), *Development in Training in Social Services*, National Institute for Social Work

Secretaries of State for Health, Social Security, Wales and Scotland (1989), *Caring for People, Community Care in the Next Decade and Beyond*, HMSO

Tizzard B (1991), in Moss and Melhuish (eds), *Current Issues in Day Care*

Vernon J, Smith C (1994), *Day nurseries at a Crossroads. Meeting the Challenge of Childcare in the Nineties*, National Children's Bureau, London